Getting Evangelicals Saved

PARIS REIDHEAD

Getting Evangelicals Saved

PARIS REIDHEAD

BETHANY HOUSE PUBLISHERS

MINNEAPOLIS, MINNESOTA 55438

A Division of Bethany Fellowship, Inc.

Copyright © 1989
Paris Reidhead
All Rights Reserved

Published by Bethany House Publishers
A Division of Bethany Fellowship, Inc.
6820 Auto Club Road, Minneapolis, Minnesota 55438

Printed in the United States of America

Library of Congress Cataloging-in-Publication Data

Reidhead, Paris.
   Getting evangelicals saved / Paris Reidhead.
      p. cm.

    1. Salvation. 2. Christian life—Christian and Missionary
Alliance authors.   I. Title.
BT751.2.R35   1989   CIP
234—dc20   89—35541
ISBN 1-55661-073-4

Dedication

Miss Elsie Born, my seventh and eighth grade teacher, shared with me the difference between "knowing the answers to all the questions" and being born of God. She is the one who first told me that when a person truly becomes a Christian, "Christ comes into his heart, and he knows it because the Spirit of God tells him to call Almighty God 'Abba, Father' " (Galatians 4:4–8).

After a career as a teacher helping boys and girls like me, Elsie was a missionary for over forty years to the Navajo Indians, serving in Farmington, New Mexico. Now at ninety years of age, the radiance of her life and testimony continues to bless her neighbors and friends.

I shall always thank God for the few brief years He sent Elsie Born to Earle Brown School, District 118 in North Minneapolis, to be my principal and teacher.

About the Author

PARIS REIDHEAD has ministered as a pastor in rural Minnesota, a linguist and missionary along the Sudan-Ethiopia border, an inner-city pastor in New York City, a consultant for the United Nations Industrial Development Organization to villages in South America and Africa, and in conference ministry for the Christian and Missionary Alliance. His life has been devoted to communicating the gospel throughout the world.

Contents

Acknowledgement

For nearly twenty years I have known and appreciated the lives and testimonies of Mr. and Mrs. Nicholas Yurchak. They have been loyal friends who have faithfully encouraged and prayed for me and the ministry the Lord has entrusted to me.

Mrs. Katherine Yurchak, who for many years worked professionally as a writer, has really been the one who made this book possible. I prayed over, worked at, and preached forth the messages that form the basis for this book. Katherine Yurchak prayed over, worked over, and edited out the problems in the manuscript copies of these messages in a most excellent manner, ever respecting and protecting the biblical substance, spiritual impact, and my personal style.

For the more than two hundred hours of dedicated time and caring effort that Katherine Yurchak so freely poured into this book, I am deeply grateful.

Paris W. Reidhead

Preface

I once was asked by evangelist Leonard Ravenhill, author of *Why Revival Tarries* and many
other books, to take his place at a conference to
be held at Bethany Fellowship in Minneapolis. I
had no idea what Bethany Fellowship was. I had
been reared in Minnesota, but there had been no
such thing as Bethany Fellowship at that time.

I was met at the airport by Duane Lovestrand
and his two sons who told me of their vision for
Bethany.

We met for our Bible conference in an unfin-
ished lounge which had no covering on the
walls—just rough insulation—but the presence of
the Lord was with us. For me it was a time of
great spiritual blessing.

Pastor T. A. Hegre, founder and director of
Bethany Fellowship, took me downstairs to a
place that seemed more like a large closet than a
room. With something of an apology, he said:
"This is our printing department." It consisted of
one used Multilith machine.

Whether it was vision or dream—or just plain
boldness—I heard myself saying to my friends at

Bethany, "Someday you're going to have five acres under roof. You will be one of the nation's largest publishers of Christian literature."

That was 1954. Today Bethany House Publishers *has* become an international leader in the publication of evangelical literature.

How I thank God for Bethany. What a blessing they have been to me and my family. And now I am grateful to Him for making possible the publication of this book, *Getting Evangelicals Saved.*

———

Some years ago, in New York City, God led me to give a series of messages on what I then called, "So Great Salvation." Later, I was at Bethany Fellowship for a Victorious Life Conference, and Pastor Hegre asked if he could use a portion of my teachings for his magazine, *The Message of the Cross.* My secretary's notes and the transcripts from the messages given at the conference were subsequently published in a little booklet which was distributed for many years.

The Spirit of God has burdened me again with this topic, the nature of salvation, because throughout the body of Christ I find the term "salvation" generally being reduced and limited to mean the forgiveness of sins, or the new birth.

By limiting this marvelous provision of God's love in Christ, we rob ourselves of everything else God has intended to be ours. We prevent Him from accomplishing for us all He intended to do through Christ's death. Because of our ignorance and indifference, we could be accused of treading under our feet what Jesus purchased for us with His precious blood. My purpose is, first of all, to help you understand the true meaning and necessity of godly repentance and, secondly, to show you how to take part in the abundant life that flows from the throne of God.

Some readers—including many who have "said the sinner's prayer," or "gone forward" in response to an altar call—may be in for a surprise. You may find yourself awakening, perhaps for the first time, to the fact that while you "accepted Christ" as your personal Savior, you have never repented of sin or come to an active, real faith in Jesus Christ, who is our Lord and Master. If that is so, do not despair.

Instead, allow the Holy Spirit to give you true conviction about your spiritual state. Then ask for His grace to work in you, leading you to the new life that God has ordained for you. For He has called us to riches in Christ Jesus, and to a great salvation!

God, who at sundry times and in divers manners spake in time past unto the fathers by the prophets, hath in these last days spoken unto us by his Son, whom he hath appointed heir of all things, by whom also he made the worlds (Hebrews 1:1–2).

Therefore we ought to give the more earnest heed to the things which we have heard, lest at any time we should let them slip. For if the word spoken by angels was stedfast, and every transgression and disobedience received a just recompence of reward, how will we escape, if we neglect so great salvation; which at the first began to be spoken by the Lord, and was confirmed unto us by them that heard him (Hebrews 2:1–3).

FATHER,

We thank and praise You for giving to us this marvelous gift of life. We're grateful for life at any time. But to be alive in the last decade of this century, with so many tools with which to serve You— and with so many privileges which never have been accorded to other generations—is truly wonderful. Because You are with us, Father, we are asking that the tremendous investment You have made in us through the poured-out life of the Lord Jesus Christ will be brought to the fullest possible measure. May it be, our God, that through this writing, decisions will be made in hearts and lives which will mean that "the Lamb who was slain" shall receive a fuller measure of the reward for His suffering than might otherwise have been. For this we give You praise in the worthy Name of the Lord Jesus Christ.

Amen.

INTRODUCTION

Christianity

A View of the High Places

A friend of mine in New York City used to be an avid collector of antique glass. He was an expert at distinguishing ancient objects from modern mass-produced pieces and would spend weekends browsing through the shops searching for treasures. He told me that some merchants had no idea of the value of the glass he purchased.

This friend was trained to know the real from the counterfeit, and that was the secret of his success. Real antique glass, he told me, always bore a mark embossed into it. By that mark, he said he could decipher when the object was made, the country of its origin and even the artist who created it.

When the law changed, requiring that only a paper tab be applied to foreign glass objects exported to the United States, my friend immediately stopped collecting. He told me that clever and deceitful craftsmen are able to produce imitation glass objects that are virtually indistinguishable from ancient works of art. Even evidences of aging, according to my friend, are worked into the glass through a sophisticated way of applying chemicals. Since the law no longer requires that the exporter produce evidence that an object is authentic, the market is now flooded with fakes.

My friend has kept all of the antique glass treasures he purchased before the change in the law, because he knows what he has is real. But he doesn't even browse in antique shops anymore. He knows the glass objects they're offering bear none of the distinguishing hallmarks of the ancient originators.

"They make them so the untrained eye can't tell the difference between the real and the genuine," he says. "I don't want to waste my time with these dealers who want to sell junk."

Personally, I know nothing about antique glass. But God has given me some insight into the marvels of His grace in making a saint out of a sinner. And during more than forty years spent in service to the Lord I have come to realize that the mass-produced product now passing for "Christian" bears little or no resemblance to the powerful reality of Christ that can and must be the hallmark of every true child of God.

In various books and periodicals, evangelical

writers are appealing for answers to this problem. *Charisma and Christian Life* magazine recently printed a feature by a missionary who asks: "Why are the Christians so ineffective today?" He continues, "With all of the accumulated knowledge we have of the Scriptures and church history and counseling and psychology and psychiatry and everything else, many Christians are still trying to be heroes along paths God has not led them."

In his book *The Twilight of a Great Civilization*, Carl F. Henry makes this observation: "We are so steeped in the anti-Christ philosophy, namely, that success consists in embracing not the values of the Sermon on the Mount, but an infinity of material things, of sex and status—that we little sense how much of what we possess of a practical Christianity really is an apostate compromise with the spirit of this age."

And John F. MacArthur, Jr., writes: "Much of contemporary evangelism is woefully deficient in confronting people with the reality of their sin."

He continues, in his book *The Gospel According to Jesus,* "Preachers offer people happiness, joy, fulfillment and all things positive. Present-day Christians are taught that all they have to do is find a person's psychological needs, then offer Jesus as a panacea for whatever the problem is. It is very easy to get a response, because people are looking for quick solutions to their felt needs."

This is no new concern among evangelicals.

More than thirty years ago, A. W. Tozer wrote a book in which he expressed "a sorrowful concern for the spiritual welfare of the church." He said, "The failure in current evangelism lies in its humanistic approach." He described much of the activity among Christians of that day as "motion without progress."

Now, three decades later, many evangelical leaders are facing the truth of Dr. Tozer's words. We know that the decline in effectiveness among Christians has been, and continues to be, steady and swift.

We have reached a critical point in evangelism today and we need to admit that something is wrong—wrong *with* us and *in* us. God's Word says that Jesus Christ has not changed and never will (Hebrews 13:8). So it is time we looked deep into our own hearts for answers to our ineffectiveness as witnesses in the world around us concerning the reality of Christ.

Those at the forefront of evangelical circles today need to hear the echo of God's words spoken through Ezekiel long ago: "The diseased have ye not strengthened, neither have ye healed that which was sick, neither have ye bound up that which was broken, neither have ye brought again that which was driven away, neither have ye sought that which was lost" (Ezekiel 34:4).

In my visits to churches I've encountered many individuals who quickly moved into religious circles after their favorite evangelist told them, "Be sure to go to church on Sunday." They made "a decision for Christ," and now are active in programs that keep them busy—but they are not blessed. Others I've met boldly confess that they "grew up Christian" and are following the tradition of their Christian parents and regularly attending church. "After all," they tell me, "we were taught that going to church is the right thing to do."

For many people in our churches these days, salvation is all in their minds. This will result in their missing heaven by eighteen inches, because God's salvation has never gotten down from their heads into their hearts, where Christ can become their life. They know the verses, but they do not know Him; whom to know is life eternal.

It is little wonder then that many are disillusioned with Christianity. They have yet to realize that salvation is *not* a plan, *not* in scripture verses, *not* in ordinances and *not* in a scheme of theology. Salvation is *not* a decision and *not* a pronouncement of an evangelist, a pastor or a teacher.

We shouldn't wonder that Christianity is not "working" for some people. God's purpose is not simply to give us a ticket to heaven. "Something's wrong, Paris," a faithful church worker confided to me. "I can't point to any*one* or any*thing*. I do my best, but it's never enough. I feel so empty— even lonely."

There are many believers in Christ who truly

want to live up to their commitment to the Lord. Even with their best effort, however, they find that Christianity is not the life-transforming, freeing venture they expected when they first embarked on their journey. This is true for many church leaders, missionaries, and countless men and woman in the pews. Many of these honest folks are saying what Oswald Chambers said before he met God in a powerful way: "If what I presently possess is all the Christianity there is, the thing is a fraud."

But the truth is, God has purposed to bring the *atmosphere*, the *government*, and the *blessing* of heaven to our hearts. Moreover, He wants to bring to us the Person who will make heavenly the here and now. Because salvation is Christ himself. He is our salvation. He is our life.

The Christian faith is based on the cardinal truth that salvation is not giving mental assent to a set of doctrinal statements: Salvation is a *Person*—Jesus Christ. Misunderstanding this point has created a generation of disillusioned and ineffective Christians. Christ did not *send* us salvation, He died to *become* our salvation.

If we admitted the truth, we evangelicals would recognize that we have dethroned the Holy Spirit—who is the only person of the Godhead in the world today, having been assigned by God to carry out His plan of salvation for mankind.

Charles Spurgeon declared, "If we have not the Spirit of God, it would be better to shut the churches, to nail up the doors, to put a black cross on them and say, 'God have mercy on us!' "

And so I want to encourage you, just as Paul exhorted the church at Corinth: "Examine yourselves, whether ye be in the faith; prove your own selves. Know ye not your own selves, how that Jesus Christ is in you, except ye be reprobates?" (2 Corinthians 13:5).

Did you know that no one in the Bible claimed he was "saved"? Paul expressed his new inner life this way: "When it pleased God to reveal His Son in me." But no one in the early church ever used the word "saved" in declaring his personal testimony. I believe they sensed that "salvation" is such an immense word that there would be no particular place or time in the Christian's pilgrimage when all that the word implies could be fulfilled by one man living and walking in time.

It is the misunderstanding and misuse of the word "saved" which, over the generations, has misled good church people into thinking that the only thing God is interested in is getting them signed up to occupy a mansion in His eternal housing development. Many of us have the idea that all God wants is for people to be fixed up with a hell-insurance policy. And so the word "salvation" has been compressed to mean the equivalent of *forgiven*. Ideas like these are not defensible from the Word of God; they are, at worst, utter misconceptions and, at best, grossly incomplete ideas about God's "so great salvation."

God's salvation will carry us to the glorious heights of transfiguration where we become like Christ. (See 2 Corinthians 3:7–18.)

Tracing the various word forms of "salvation" through the New Testament, we find the verb has four tenses: (the perfect tense), I have been saved from the *pleasure* of sin, which is repentance; (the past tense), I was saved from the *penalty* of sin, which is justification; (the present tense), I am being saved from the *power* of sin which is sanctification and; (the future tense), I shall be saved from the *presence* of sin which is glorification.

To explain the broadness of salvation, Paul says, "... for now is our salvation nearer than when we believed" (Romans 13:11). Again, he says, "For if, when we were enemies, we were reconciled to God by the death of his Son, much more, being reconciled, we shall be saved by his life" (Romans 5:10).

In God's mind, our salvation was accomplished by Jesus Christ at Calvary. *Potentially*, salvation became ours at the point of repentance. *Experientially*, it is ours when we see ourselves in union with Christ. *Effectively*, this salvation will be ours through the endless ages of eternity. This hardly gives us a view of salvation that can be reduced to a formula, or a prayer uttered at one moment in time. We have before us a view of the heights of heaven—and of ourselves transformed into new creations!

But like every journey, there is a first step.

Repentance is the only means whereby the barrier between you and God can be removed; that His grace may bring you into *fellowship with Him.* This is a salvation far beyond just wanting God to take you to heaven. For if God were to send you to heaven—if He would give you a house on the main street of Glory, or if He were to furnish you a home next to the River of Life—God still would have doomed you to hell. Because heaven is not heaven, if He is not there. The thing that makes heaven heavenly is not the mansion, or the streets of gold, or the River of Life, or the angels playing their harps—it is the revelation of God without restriction or inhibition or anything else to obscure Him. Heaven is heavenly because of the presence of the King of that place—the Lord Jesus Christ.

God, in His grace, longs to make us like Jesus Christ. He has purposed, by His Grace, to bring us into a living, warm fellowship with Him *now*, in this very day of our earthly pilgrimage. Then, because He already has brought heaven *to* us, it is a simple matter for Him later to take us to that place He has prepared for us. The "so great salvation" He desires for us is to have heaven begin in our hearts today.

In Hebrews 2, the Holy Spirit asks, "How shall we escape if we ignore . . ." This is not refusal, not rejection, not a matter of taking a stand against. It is just a little matter of saying, "Another day . . . another time. There are things more important to me just now—some things more challenging—interests more demanding of my time and attention."

But how are you going to explain the sin of neglect to your heavenly Father? How are you going to face Him who purchased the many priceless privileges for you with the precious blood of Christ?

I once met a young man who said to me, "Christianity and salvation are okay for people when they're on their last leg. But anyone as young as I am doesn't want to be saddled with a lot of do's and don'ts. When I get old enough to claim my social security, I'll also take out my heavenly security."

I said to him, "Fine. I'll draw up a contract and you can sign it."

His mother handed me a piece of paper and I began to write something like this: *Because I do not know that I will live to be old enough to take my social security, and because I have no certainty of tomorrow, and because I have made up my mind that I am not going to do anything with Jesus Christ until I get to be at least sixty-five years old, I hereby relinquish all interest in the death of Christ.*

I declare to one and sundry to whom this paper may come that I refuse hereafter to consider myself a candidate for salvation. I am determined, therefore, to go to hell. I have made up my mind that I shall be lost, if lostness is a consequence of my ac-

tion, *because I simply am not interested in Jesus Christ.*

Then I asked the young man, "Would you sign this paper?"

After reading the contract, his face blanched. "No, I won't sign that," he protested. "Do you think I'm a fool?"

"Yes, I do," I replied. "Because, essentially, you *have* signed it by telling your mother, your wife and all of us here that it's your intention to do nothing with Jesus Christ until some indefinite point in the future. You might as well get the thing off your mind. Then, when people trouble you in the future, you can tell them you've settled it. You can say to them, 'One Sunday afternoon, in my mother's home, I made up my mind I wasn't going to be bothered about salvation anymore.' "

What happened to that young man? I do not know. Nonetheless, it is my conviction that hell is filled with people who have said: "Someday . . . someday."

I'm not promoting the idea that evangelists should pass around pieces of paper on which people have to write statements either affirming or denying their belief in Jesus Christ. By His very life, Jesus demonstrated God's love toward *repentant* sinners. He personally mingled freely among publicans and flagrant sinners, drawing the hatred of the Pharisees against himself. But not a single penitent soul who has gone to Him has ever been denied His divine compassion.

We have His own words to assure us: "I say unto you, that likewise joy shall be in heaven over one sinner that repenteth, more than over ninety and nine just persons, which need no repentance" (Luke 15:7).

It is fatal to neglect repentance and faith! We have every reason to believe that "the Lord Jesus shall be revealed from heaven with his mighty angels, in flaming fire taking vengeance on them that know not God, and that obey not the gospel of our Lord Jesus Christ" (2 Thessalonians 1:7–8). Included in that company of people will be those who simply have neglected to repent. So while it is of tremendous importance to acknowledge Jesus Christ as Savior, it is equally important to take the other precious things He purchased for you through His death.

Some have the erroneous idea that God has His first-class citizens and second-class citizens; that the important thing is to get people "saved." Then if somebody wants to move on to "the deeper life," "the higher life," "the fuller life," or "the sanctified life,"—well, that's up to them. But *everything* God provided through the Lord Jesus in His work on the cross is important. That's why the Spirit of God insists, "How shall we escape, if we neglect" anything God intended to be ours?

In a parable, Jesus taught about a king who sent out many invitations to a great banquet. (See Luke 14:16–24.) One of those invited refused because, he said, his new real estate acquisition required him to go and manage it. Another was also busy buying and selling and said he had to take care of his financial interests. Still another man had domestic interests which resulted in his refusal of the king's invitation.

So whether it is real estate, building a bankroll, or one's sensual desires for comfort (and it may be many other things), the application of this parable to our hearts says to the listening soul that the world is too much with us these days.

In His parable, Jesus pointed out that the worldly heart is not compatible with the heavenly riches God has planned for His own.

Let's suppose you have been justified by faith in Christ, but have gone through this life with complete indifference to the rest of God's so great salvation. Let's imagine that you arrive in heaven and God greets you with the words: "Come with me, my child." He takes you to the warehouse of His Grace, throws back the big double doors and reveals to you deep shelves lined with the marvelous things He had purchased for you with the precious blood of His beloved Son. As you survey the packages on the shelves, you see He has signed, sealed and addressed them to you with the promise that they would reach you at various stages in your earthly pilgrimage. With trembling hands, you unwrap one of the packages that has remained on eternity's shelf. In it you discover *health* you could have had during that time of debilitating illness.

There's another package filled with *victory* that might have been yours in that time when you were struggling with temptation. Also on the shelf is a large crate loaded with the *power* of the Holy Spirit that might have been yours when you'd been entrusted with a special task.

As tears flow unchecked down your cheeks, you will hear God the Father say: "Why, my child, did you not take victory? Why didn't you claim my power for you? I made full provision for you every step of the way."

In a flashback of your life, God will show you how you went along broken and defeated, how you crept, when you could have run; how you could have stopped crawling as a worm in the dust and mounted up as an eagle.

Then, in a glimpse of what your life *might* have been, He will show you the many blessings you could have known had you not spent your earthly days in neglect.

He will reveal to you that you were too calloused to claim the provisions that had been so generously offered you through the sacrifice of His Son, your Savior. How will you escape the heartache and grief that comes from realizing you have denied the Lord Jesus the glory He could have gotten out of your life?

If only you had cared about the provisions of

His love! If only you had not been satisfied with a crumb when He wanted you to have a whole loaf. In that day, you'll see not only how you missed personal blessing, but how you dishonored Him throughout your lifetime—how you were less than He called you to be, because you neglected the riches of His salvation.

But now!—you *are* alive and privileged to have a fresh opportunity to discover, maybe for the first time, the riches of God's grace. I feel privileged, too—privileged and obliged to help you discover God's so great salvation!

The Solid Rock

My hope is built on nothing less
Than Jesus' blood and righteousness;
I dare not trust the sweetest frame,
But wholly lean on Jesus' name.
On Christ the solid Rock, I stand—
All other ground is sinking sand,
All other ground is sinking sand.

—Edward Mote

ONE

Conversion

What Jesus Says About Salvation

The Bible says that "in these last days [God has] spoken unto us by his Son" (Hebrews 1:2). Don't you think it would be wise to discover what it is Jesus Christ says to us about His Father's great salvation?

In Matthew 5:20, Jesus spoke to a company of people about the most important subject in the world: "For I say unto you, That except your righteousness shall exceed the righteousness of the scribes and Pharisees, ye shall in no case enter into the kingdom of heaven."

What was the righteousness of the Pharisees and teachers of the law? It was a righteousness which the most dedicated mind and consecrated intellect could produce *without the Holy Spirit.* The scribes and Pharisees fasted, tithed, prayed, abstained from eating meat, observed holy days, and memorized scripture. They were most enthusiastic in discussions about their religion. Anyone can do all these things without the enablement of the Holy Spirit.

This says something of drastic importance to you and me: We can be orthodox in our theology, evangelistic in our zeal, missionary in our fervor, and devout in the practice of our religion; we can fast, tithe and pray—all with our natural energy. But that's the same energy with which you previously served the Devil.

The Lord Jesus Christ says that the righteousness which prepares you for heaven is not produced with your own energy. The righteousness produced in us must be from another source entirely. The Lord wants His disciples to know that the righteousness which is from above results from the work of God in you.

Jesus spoke often about this new way of entering the life of the Spirit. He called it *repentance*—which is ceasing from trying to earn salvation man's way and learning how to please God daily. In Luke 13:3–5, He says, ". . . except ye repent, ye shall all likewise perish."

I must ask: Have you repented of your sin? Or have you neglected repentance? Without repentance sinners cannot escape God's wrath.

Repentance is defined by the Scripturse as a change of mind, turning away from the intention and purpose of pleasing self and choosing to please God. The seed of all righteousness and holiness is in repentance. Perhaps a man's purpose—his aim and direction—is to please himself. But when he repents he must make an about-face. This is a complete turnabout.

From that moment on, the intention of this man is to please and glorify God—to satisfy only Him. The salvation of which Jesus speaks is not our being satisfied with Him, rather it is His being satisfied with us. Can you see how fatal it is to neglect the salvation that comes in repentance?

In Matthew 18:3, we get a picture of the Lord walking with His disciples. They have been arguing about which one of them will be the greatest in the kingdom of heaven. To illustrate His point, Jesus called a little child and set him on His knee. Then he turned to His disciples and said, "Except ye be converted, and become as little children, ye shall not enter into the kingdom of heaven."

The word for *change* in the King James Version is that good Bible word "converted," which means "turn again." The Lord Jesus was saying this to His disciples: Though you've repented—received and believed me—the evidence of the genuineness of my work in your heart is that every time your mind is in conflict with my mind, it must be my mind that prevails, just as a little child must accept the will of his parents.

This is the reason for Paul's exhortation. "And

be not conformed to this world: but be ye transformed by the renewing of your mind" (Romans 12:2).

Many of the things we carry into the life of forgiveness and pardon are not ordained of God and not according to His will. Therefore, at every step of our pilgrimage, when we find some sinful attitude in conflict with what His holiness prescribes, the evidence of a genuine work of God in our heart is that we turn again—we are *converted*—so that His way prevails.

For example, let's say you are about to make a certain wrong choice or enter a wrong relationship—you are set on a direction He has allowed (not commanded) you to go. But suddenly, the Spirit of God stops you. His voice in your heart says, "You *cannot* go that way." If you are His child, you will turn again and go in the way He leads.

Conversion is the attitude of correcting wrong things in the day-to-day Christian life. Suppose you have decided to drive from Minneapolis to New York City. The first thing you need to do is to head in the right direction—east. But even after you've decided to go east, you can't just lock your wheels and step on the gas. All along the way, there will be tens of thousands of minute course corrections. As you drive along there may be a slant in the road and so you will need to correct the wheels to allow for it.

As believers in Jesus Christ, we have a new

tendency in our disposition—in our nature. Our purpose is to please God, and the evidence of the genuineness of His work in our hearts is that whenever we sense a drift toward that which is not of God—whenever we know something in us that is not pleasing Him—we make a correction in our course. By an act of our will we turn again from whatever would pull us into a ditch.

Conversion, then, means to have an attitude of constant correction from our will to the will of God, a continuous concern that we will please Him in all we do. This is not just the fact that at some point in our past we may have signed a decision card. Today—this very moment—the attitude of our heart must be: I want to please God.

If He shows you some action or attitude, anything you're doing that does not please Him, don't neglect the opportunity He gives for immediate deliverance. Don't rest in the past. Don't fall into the sin of neglect. Move continuously toward His will, and say in your heart, "Lord, I want to please You today as much as the day when I first met You."

The Lord Jesus continues to speak to us of His so great salvation in John chapter 3. Three times, in as many verses, he says, "Except a man be born again, he cannot see the kingdom of God" (v. 3). And, "Except a man be born of water sand of the Spirit, he cannot enter into the kingdom of God" (v. 5). And again, "Ye must be born again" (v. 7).

Our Lord Jesus could not have made it more

clear. What *prepares* us for salvation, He says, is not some action or movement we make toward God, but an action God has made toward us. His initial call to us, through the Holy Spirit, is a love-gift.

Before we lose our way here, however, you must understand that there is something we must do toward God, following the Holy Spirit's wooing. We must repent. We must believe. And the evidence of the genuineness of repentance and faith is this: When you repent and believe, God regenerates you by His Holy Spirit and gives the witness of the Spirit within your heart that you have passed from death to life. He lets us know, without a shadow of a doubt, that we have been born again.

It is fatal to commit the sin of neglect at this point! Be absolutely certain you repent, turning away constantly from the righteousness that is produced by our human effort, and turning toward the righteousness produced by God through the sovereign and supernatural work of the Holy Spirit.

You may well ask, "How is this accomplished?"

In the gospel of John, the Lord spoke to a company of people who would make Him king. They wanted to be His disciples, but they asked Him for some certification, a credential—a miracle, for instance—that would prove He was who He said He was.

He responded:

"Whoso eateth my flesh, and drinketh my blood, hath eternal life; and I will raise him up at the last day" (John 6:48–54).

So salvation is not just Christ on the cross, or Christ in the tomb, but Christ raised from the dead, ascended to the throne and pouring His eternal life back into you and me. It is "Christ in you, the hope of glory" (Colossians 1:27). It is He, becoming so united with the believer that it is as we have eaten His flesh and drunk His blood. He has become bone of our bone and life of our life. He has joined himself to us and we have received Him. Salvation is not *from* Him, salvation is *in* Him. He wants to be in you—to be your life. This is the testimony of the Word.

So if Christianity has not been meeting your high expectations, I encourage you to investigate your own heart. Is it possible you have neglected something God has been trying to have you know? Can you say, "Christ the Lord *is* my salvation"? That truth was clear to David, who exclaimed in Psalm 27:1, "The Lord [Jehovah] is my light and my salvation."

You see, Christ is not our Savior because He is in heaven. He is our salvation when He lives in us.

Just as Jesus spoke to those Jews, He will continue to speak to us in these last days, something else about this so great salvation:

> Verily, verily, I say unto you, Except a corn of wheat fall into the ground and die, it abideth alone: but if it die, it bringeth forth much fruit. He that loveth his life shall lose it; and he that hateth his life in this world shall keep it unto life eternal. If any man serve me, let him follow me; and where I am, there shall also my servant be: if any man serve me, him will my Father honour (John 12:24–26).

This so great salvation, which He purchased for us at such great price, insists on our following Him.

Where did the Lord Jesus go for us? He went to the cross and was crucified in our place and in our stead. Like a kernel of wheat, He "fell to the ground and died," knowing that if He did not suffer crucifixion He would remain but a single seed. He knew the Father had sent Him into the world for that hour and purpose. And so He had to die on the cross to produce many new seeds. And those who believe in Him and live in this world as He lived are the fruit of His love.

It is important for you to understand that our Lord, in His earthly ministry, mentioned the word "cross" only four times and it was always mentioned in reference to His disciples.

To the Twelve He said, "And he that taketh not his cross, and followeth after me, is not worthy of me" (Matthew 10:38).

Speaking to the rich young ruler, whom He instructed to sell all his possessions, He said, ". . . come, take up the cross, and follow me" (Mark 10:21).

And on two other occasions, Jesus made it plain that "whosoever doth not bear his cross, and come after me, cannot be my disciple" (see especially Luke 14:27).

People could not understand what our Lord was saying then, and Christians today do not understand what the word *cross* means when Jesus used it in this context. Taking up the cross—that is, by daily identifying with His death—we are not only delivered from sin and hell, but it also means being delivered from the bondage of the world in which we live. This world governs and controls us. It forms our attitudes, fills our heads with its maxims, and enslaves us by tantalizing us with its rewards and alluring interests. Taking up the cross includes salvation from our own personality, nature, traits and habits—and from those fleshly attitudes we've developed that make our hearts cold and dead to God's Spirit.

When we live *in* Christ, we also experience deliverance from the Devil. We were his bondslaves, since he was given control of our lives—first, by the father of the race, and later confirmed by us through our own choice when you and I reached the age of accountability. As children of the Devil, we exhibited his nature, performed his acts and accepted his government.

But now we have come to Jesus Christ, whose purpose is also to save us from the Devil, with all of his power and cunning and craftiness. The Lord Jesus died to set us free. "If the Son therefore shall make you free, ye shall be free indeed" (John 8:36).

Will we allow our concern and interest to be fixed on worldly things that are more appealing to the human heart? Or will we accept the heavenly treasures that have been purchased for us at the tremendous price of the blood of Christ?

Today, you have heard the voice of the Lord concerning the length, breadth, height and depth of the salvation offered to you. Perhaps you feel a new stirring within. Perhaps what you are feeling is the awakening of your soul to truths that you may be seeing for the first time.

Awakening is, itself, the first step in the spiritual pilgrimage. And it's to this subject we must now direct our attention as we go step by step in our look at the "so great a salvation" that Jesus offers.

Jesus' View of Salvation:

1. In your own words, define what it means to repent.
2. Why is it essential for conversion?
3. What part does our human will play in repentance?
4. Is repentance a one-time act or is it something

we do continually? Explain.

5. What does it mean to eat Christ's flesh and drink His blood? Does the explanation given in this chapter differ with your previous understanding of this command?

6. Has the Lord given you an awareness of any areas of your life—inner attitudes or outward actions—that are not pleasing to Him?

7. What is your understanding about Jesus' exhortation, "Take up your cross daily and follow Me"?

Open My Eyes, That I May See

Open my eyes, that I may see
Glimpses of truth Thou hast for me;
Place in my hands the wonderful key
That shall unclasp and set me free.
Silently now I wait for Thee,
Ready my God, Thy will to see;
Open my heart illumine me,
Spirit divine!

—Clara H. Scott

TWO

Awakening:

Some Training for Surgical Nurses

Perhaps you have been wondering at some of my strong statements about the true gospel of our Lord—the need for repentance, and for taking on yourself the death and new life of the Holy Spirit. If so, it is little wonder. For more than a century, a thick darkness has been trying to settle itself over the light that shines from God's Word.

Let me give you a brief history.

———

In the middle of the nineteenth century, a conflict arose in Europe among seminary professors who were influenced by Charles Darwin and the German philosopher Nietzsche. Some began applying their principles of skepticism to the Word of God, so that they questioned the fact of its divine inspiration. They said it was by an evolutionary process that we received the Scriptures. The virgin birth of Christ came into question because it was not "scientific." His sinless life, atoning death, bodily resurrection and ascension—all these were suspect.

We call such men as these "theorists," "modernists," or "liberals." During that time, however, many men in our American seminaries, who were preparing to be professors, went to Europe to finish their education. And they certainly came back to the United States "finished." Upon returning, those professors succeeded in corrupting students enrolled in our American seminaries, and the consequence has been open warfare against the truth of God.

This conflict caused one of Charles Spurgeon's parishioners to plead, "Pastor, you've got to do something about this terrible heresy they're preaching. You must defend the Bible against these men!"

But Pastor Spurgeon, with characteristic insight, replied, "Oh no I don't. The Bible, with its gospel, is a lion. Just turn it loose. It will take care of itself."

While the Word of God, indeed, never needs any man's defense, the fact is those heresies did *penetrate* our seminaries. Yet, among the people of God there were certain truths considered to be essential to the faith. These we call "fundamental truths." And those who accepted these truths were genuinely and wonderfully born of God!

However, when their children grew to adulthood, these beliefs were being adulterated. Many thought: If you merely believe in the fundamentals—that is, if you say, "yes, these basic doctrinal propositions of Christianity are true"—you can assume you are saved.

With the third, fourth and fifth generations—where we stand today—the gospel has been increasingly obscured. What we find today in Christian circles is this: If you will say, "Uh-huh," to these few questions you are hereby declared "saved."

This practice led the pastor of a large church in Memphis to make a bold statement once before the Southern Baptist Convention at Spartansburg, South Carolina. He declared that, based on his forty years of close observation in the churches, probably no more than one out of ten of the Southern Baptists experientially knew anything about the new birth.

Later, a group of noted theologians prepared a book they entitled *Contemporary Evangelical Thought* which was edited by Carl F. Henry. Reporting the findings of a survey among one evangelical denomination, they wrote that 20% of the members never prayed; 25% never read the Bible, 30% never attended the church school, 90% never had family prayers, 95% never gave the tithe, and 95% had never invited a person to become a Christian.

An Episcopal professor of theology wrote in a

popular periodical after a survey of church conditions across the country: "One can hardly offer statistics on a matter of the sort, but it would not be far wrong to say that perhaps 5% of the 70 or 80 million church members among the 150 million Americans have some real grasp of what their faith means; and that appears to be a generous estimate."

He went on to say: "I estimate that 10% of our Protestant church members are reasonably well informed and that 25% are living up to their limited light. But, 'what are these among so many?' Even with my more optimistic surmise, where does this leave a typical local church? As at Laodicea of old (Revelation 3:14–19); in need of a revival, and of pastoral nurture!"[1]

When I was a pastor at the Gospel Tabernacle in New York City, we were visited frequently by the late Dr. A. W. Tozer. He made the same sad observation: "Among evangelical churches—including the society of which I am part—probably no more than one out of ten know anything experientially about the new birth."

It is not my intention to prove any of these men right or wrong. What I am saying is that we have been living through decades of what is

---

[1]Blackwood, Andrew W. *Contemporary Evangelical Thought*, ed. Carl F. Henry, (Great Neck, N.Y.: Channel Press, 1957), 295.

known as "easy believism." Consequently, many people in the churches of America have everything but *life*. Included in these churches are the old-line denominational and evangelical groups, as well as several of the more recent movements. A beautiful "plan" is being presented, but it is built upon sand—not upon the Rock, which is **CHRIST JESUS.**

Now I, for one, want to see this pattern changed. So when I heard Willard Scott say recently on the "Today" show that the fastest growing group in America is comprised of people over one hundred years of age, I immediately put in my application. I've asked the Lord to "renew my youth like the eagle's." Because if we're going to serve the Lord for the balance of this century and into the next century, we've got to recognize that the message of salvation must not be addressed only to "the world," but to members of America's evangelical churches also. The greatest field for evangelism today, and in the days ahead, is among church members.

Even now, we are beginning to see the effects of ministering to the churches. For example, a man who for eleven years was an elder in an Alliance Church was suddenly born of God. A woman who was the head of the Women's Mission Society of the Southern Baptist Convention testified that she, too, was newly born of God. At Tacoa Falls Bible Institute, a graduate student who for years was a minister of music there, declared publicly that he was just born of God.

Do you understand the gravity of what I am telling you? These men and women had been in churches many years. It is our duty, therefore, to tell others like them what God wants to do for them—that He would begin the process of bringing them out of death into life.

That spiritual process in man begins with the crisis of the new birth. The new birth is followed by a process that issues into another crisis—that of the baptism of the Holy Spirit. And that crisis is followed by the process of living and walking in the Spirit. That process, in its entirety, is God's great salvation.

It begins with God's great loving purpose, reaching out to people who are still dead in their trespasses and sins. This is the beginning of spiritual *awakening*.

To accomplish this, He first assigns someone to be next to the person who is spiritually dead, in order that they will have an example of His grace.

Now some of you may sense that you are just in the awakening moments. Others of you may have been walking with the Lord for some time now. It is to this second group that I address the remarks that follow.

Did you know that for some people, the best Christian they know is you? God not only wants you to be a living example, but He will burden you to intercede for the lost individual He puts you next to. (In fact, that person might be next to you in the pew!) This is the second aspect in God's plan of spiritual awakening. If God is going to start working in the sinner's heart, it seems He will always have someone praying for his lost condition. And so intercession is a vital part of evangelism, and will become vital in your continuing walk with the Lord.

These days, it's not "popular" to talk about hell and eternal separation from God. But it is a fact that while God takes no joy in sending anyone to hell, He nonetheless gives sinful men the freedom to go there if they choose. As He said through the prophet Ezekiel:

> "Say unto them, As I live, saith the Lord God, I have no pleasure in the death of the wicked; but that the wicked turn from his way and live: turn ye, turn ye from your evil ways; for why will ye die?" (Ezekiel 33:11)

God yearns for sinners to be saved, but gives them the right to choose to die and end up in hell, because it was their own decision to have "walked according to the course of this world, according to the prince of the power of the air" (Ephesians 2:2). They have chosen to serve the Devil and live under his government. Sinners do what they want to do by choice, and God respects that right. He will not interfere—until the sinner or until the sinner's representative asks Him to intervene.

The believer's privilege of prayer is extraordinary. Consider this passage: ". . . [He] that loved us, and washed us from our sins in his own blood . . . hath made us kings and priests unto God and his Father . . ." (Revelation 1:5–6).

God did not say, "By the way, if you ever run out of interesting things to do, would you mind giving a little thought and attention to the possibility of being a priest and interceding for a sinner now and then? Uh . . . I don't want to burden you, but . . ."

Not at all! He washed us in His blood and made you and me to be priests. It is a priest's responsibility and privilege to intercede. The priest-intercessor goes into the presence of God on behalf of the sinner. He confesses what the sinner ought to confess, and accepts the sinner's condemnation and guilt. The priest-intercessor is the court-appointed, legal representative for the sinner, pleading with God to begin a work of grace in the sinner's heart.

Another thing God does for the lost individual is to get somebody to witness to him. A witness is someone who tells what he has seen, heard and experienced—nothing more! Going beyond that, one becomes a philosopher, or a metaphysician. God did not say, "You will be my philosophers." He said, ". . . ye shall be witnesses" (Acts 1:8). If a witness goes beyond what he's heard and experienced, then his words are inadmissable.

How do you know whether or not you are a valid witness?

Have you heard God speak through His Word concerning His holiness and righteousness? Have you ever caught a glimpse of your own heart and seen yourself as God declares you to be—a traitor, a rebel, an anarchist, a transgressor, an enemy of the cause of Christ? Have you ever heard Jesus say to you, "Come unto Me, and rest?" Have you come? Did you find cleansing? Did you find forgiveness? Did you experience the new birth? Have you heard the witness of the Spirit inviting you to call almighty God, "Abba Father"?

Then, you *are* a witness. As a witness, you are to tell what you've seen and heard and experienced. We don't know the answers to all the questions. We don't need to know them. All we need to do is tell what God has done in and for us. That's all!

No one in the world can contradict you about yourself. If you really have had an experience, then you are an authority on you. To anyone in the world, you can say, "This is what I saw. This is what I heard. This is what I experienced." *That is witnessing*.

When you have done all that, you have done all you are able to do. Live Christ; intercede; witness to sinners. From that moment on, it is up to God to act.

It is God's work to awaken the sinner.

If you are unsure whether you have experienced the new birth—or if you are sure you have *not*—examine carefully what I am about to tell you.

The Scriptures tell us only a little about sinners. I already have listed five things we are before we come to God: traitors, rebels, anarchists, transgressors and enemies. This is because, according to the Scriptures, "The god of this world hath blinded the minds of them which believe not, lest the light of the glorious gospel of Christ, who is the image of God, should shine unto them" (2 Corinthians 4:4).

A darkened mind. People who try to take a nap in the middle of the day can't get the room dark enough, so they put on a blindfold. That's what the god of this world has done to the lost. He has darkened or blinded their minds. He did it deliberately, and quite effectively. But let's read something more about the condition of the sinner: ". . . [You] who were dead in trespasses and sins" (Ephesians 2:1).

Dead. Not only blind, but dead! There's no interest in the things of God—no sensitivity to the work and Word of God. And that's why the sinner has to be *awakened*.

The Lord says: "Awake to righteousness" (1 Corinthians 15:34). And again we read: "Awake thou that sleepest, and arise from the dead" (Ephesians 5:14).

In a conversation with a surgeon friend, he

told me that the most important person in the operating room, other than the surgeon, is the surgical nurse. The surgical nurse needs to know what procedure is to be done, which instrument is to be used and for what purpose. The surgical nurse needs to know how to pick up the scalpel and how to firmly place it in the hand of the surgeon without fumbling or dropping it.

In a sense, the believer in Christ is a "surgical nurse" to the Holy Spirit. If you find a sinner who is asleep, do you know which "scalpels" of truth are needed to effectively awaken that sinner? The Holy Spirit, the Wise Surgeon, chooses certain scriptures, which He will call into use.

Some of you who have been trained in evangelism "techniques" may be surprised at this: Please don't use John 3:16 with an unawakened sinner. Because, if you tell a sinner *how* to be saved, before he knows he *needs* to be saved, you only succeed in hardening him toward the gospel.

I don't know what Paul and Silas said during those hours they were in the Philippian jail. But I do know they did not tell the people in prison *how* to be saved. The angel of the Lord opened the prison doors and unlocked the shackles that held the apostles. But Paul and Silas did not begin preaching. They waited until the jailer asked, "What must I do to be saved?" He had been awakened. Then Paul responded to his question: "Believe on the Lord Jesus Christ, and thou shalt be saved, and thy house" (Acts 16:31).

If I had my way, I would declare a moratorium on public preaching of "the plan of salvation" in America for one to two years. Then I would call on everyone who has use of the airwaves and the pulpits to preach the *holiness* of God, the *righteousness* of God and the *law* of God, until sinners would cry out, "What must we do to be saved?" Then I would take them off in a corner and whisper the gospel to them. Such drastic action is needed because we have gospel-hardened a generation of sinners by telling them *how* to be saved before they have any understanding why they *need* to be saved.

I will suggest a few scriptures, but it is your responsibility to find others and then allow the Holy Spirit to bring them to your memory when He presents to you an unawakened sinner. He will also teach you how to use the Word and *which* word to use.

Here is a verse worth underlining and memorizing: "Surely thou didst set them in slippery places: thou castedst them down into destruction" (Psalm 73:18). This is what the Word says about the wicked. Do you think a sinner believes he is standing in slippery places?

Someone who is not awakened to the truth may well have determined in their heart that they're going to do something about God when they get older. But what does the Word of God say? That they're standing on a hillside of wet clay. They think they're walking on a flat sidewalk, but they are standing in a slippery place!

Consider, too, the next verse: "Wherefore their way shall be unto them as slippery ways in the darkness: they shall be driven on, and fall therein: for I will bring evil upon them, even the year of their visitation" (Jeremiah 23:12).

That scripture could have the effect of causing a person—one complacent in his sin and unawakened—to give his condition a little bit of thought.

Now, I need to point out something here. In evangelical circles today we find many who began their walk with the Lord in good faith, but they have become lethargic and have fallen asleep. Many believers need to be awakened by the Holy Spirit too. It may well be that, even before you equip yourself with scripture verses to awaken the lost, there is a first step to be taken. If you have been unconcerned about the lost, you can ask God to forgive you for the terrible sin of neglect—for sin it is. What I'm saying is this: If saints are not awakened to their condition—let alone to the lostness of the lost, it is going to be difficult for the church to carry out the work Christ has given us to do. I'm suggesting that we take this very personally. Whether it is a loved one, a friend, a neighbor—anyone who does not know the Lord—you and I need to be intensely interested in their lost state.

We can rest assured that when we open our hearts to God and become willing to go to the lost, the Holy Spirit will begin to reach out through us, awakening sinners in even the most unusual ways. When I was a young man, I was called to be the pastor of the First Baptist Church in Little Falls, Minnesota. At that time, a man by the name of Victor was there with his wife, Alice. On one occasion, I heard him tell of his experience in coming to the Lord.

Victor said he had gone up to Bemidji, Minnesota a rebellious young man and determined to live for himself. He enjoyed all the things his crowd did—with gusto.

Now Victor had a job, and he at least had sense enough to bring his money home to his mother when he got paid on Friday afternoon. Of course, he would keep a little bit for his own carousing, which consumed most of the weekend.

One particular Friday night, however, he had gone through all of his money and needed more. But his mother was at an evangelistic meeting in the local church. The only way to get his hands on more cash was to go to the church and be there when his mother came out.

When Victor drove into the church yard, he decided to park, get out and sit on the fender of his car. Since it was a warm summer evening, the church door was open. As Victor sat there, listening, the most remarkable thing occurred.

"For some reason," the preacher said, "I feel prompted of the Lord to stop this sermon and quote a verse of scripture." Then he quoted Proverbs 29:1: "He that being often reproved hardeneth his neck, shall suddenly be destroyed, and that without remedy."

Then the preacher said, "I feel I must give that scripture again." So he recited it a second time. He again tried to go on with his sermon, but he said, "I feel I must give that scripture a *third* time. I don't know why."

But Victor knew. The third time the preacher quoted that verse, he slid behind the wheel of his car, started it, and drove to a lonely place outside the city. He just sat there. God had spoken to his heart.

As he told it, "I opened the car door, got out and knelt on the ground. There, I opened my heart to Jesus Christ. When I drove back to my mother, I didn't go to get more money for booze. Instead, I told her that I'd been born into the family of God."

Now *that* is evidence of both the scalpel of the Word and the power of the Spirit at work through a man who was available for God to use!

For those who may be living the life of rebellion, such as Victor Earnest was living as a young man, I want to tell you something: It is foolish to play around with sin. It's dangerous and often fatal. There are examples in the Scriptures of men and women who rejected the Holy Spirit's warnings to their spirits and perished.

I am just as impressed with David, whom the Scriptures describe as "a man whose heart was toward the Lord." We find that he was found guilty of such gross sins as adultery and plotting to have his lover's husband murdered. When Nathan the prophet exposed David's sin, he was pierced in his heart and soul by the truth of those words.

For centuries, David's prayer as recorded in Psalm 51:10 has been a pattern of true humility and penitence before God: "Create in me a clean heart, O God." And he was forgiven.

We have this assurance from God's Word: "If we confess our sins, he is faithful and just to forgive us our sins, and to cleanse us from all unrighteousness" (1 John 1:9).

That is the way it is with God. Whether you are awakening to your true state for the first time—that of a rebel and traitor against God—or whether you have been cold and indifferent toward the lost, God longs for you to come to Him.

Why don't we take a moment to pray right now?

Father, should there be someone reading this who does not experientially know you "whom to know is life eternal," may this be the time when they will do something about it. For those of us who have been indifferent to the plight of the lost, God of grace, forgive us. Cleanse us from this and give us hearts of compassion—hearts that are burdened for the lost. Give us a readiness and willingness to witness to them, as you lead us and as they have need. Teach us to be skilled in the use of the Word, and to be wise in applying the truth of the Word to the hearts of men, as their need may be. To that end, Father, seal the Word in us, for Jesus' sake. Amen.

Awakening:

1. What is "easy believism" and what has caused its growth?
2. If you are a Christian, what was your salvation experience like? How did your life change?
3. What does a sinner need to know before he is taught *how* to be saved? How is this accomplished? Which type of scripture passages should you memorize?
4. What does it mean to intercede on behalf of sinners? Who is given this responsibility?
5. What does it mean to be a *witness*?
6. What does it mean to "believe *on* the Lord Jesus Christ"?

What Will You Do With Jesus?

Will you, like Peter, your Lord deny?
Or will you scorn from His foes to fly,
Daring for Jesus to live or die?
What will you do with Jesus?
What will you do with Jesus?
Neutral you cannot be;
Someday your heart will be asking,
"What will He do with me?"

—Albert B. Simpson

THREE

Conviction:

Calling It Like It Is

Nevertheless I tell you the truth; it is expedient for you that I go away: for if I go not away, the Comforter will not come unto you; but if I depart, I will send him unto you. And when he is come, he will reprove the world of sin, and of righteousness, and of judgment: of sin, because they believe not on me; of righteousness, because I go to my Father, and ye see me no more; of judgment, because the prince of this world is judged (John 16:7–11).

"Stepping up to life"—that's how Pastor Elmer Murdock, of Omaha, Nebraska, has described the various steps of the divine operation. As we go on, we will discover that everything that follows in our spiritual life is built upon all that has preceded. And after a man or woman is awakened to their lost state, God does have a second crucial step which cannot be avoided if you want to enter into His great salvation.

This second phase of the divine operation is *conviction*. If it is not clear what sin is, how will it be possible for there to be sincere conviction?

Most people you meet have already accepted their own plan of salvation—a plan which excludes the principles of God's so great salvation. We've heard people say: "God's got a big scale in the sky. He's putting all my good deeds on one side and my bad deeds on the other. If my good deeds outweigh my bad deeds, it will be alright for me." But this certainly is not based on scriptural evidence, and it will never lead to godly conviction—what the apostle Paul would call godly sorrow that leads to repentance (see 2 Corinthians 7:10).

Conviction is a legal term. In a court of law, the offender is convicted when he has been found guilty of his crimes. Spiritually, conviction is the process the Holy Spirit uses in dealing with the awakened soul.

Please note my emphasis that the *Holy Spirit* is the only authority in the world today designated by God to say to the sinner, "You're guilty!" This is an important point. We evangelicals, anxious to bring large numbers of people into our ranks, have often usurped the authority of the Third Person of the Trinity. It is His task to use whomever or whatever He wills, *as* He wills and *when* He wills to woo the sinner to come to God through Jesus Christ, who himself says it is the Holy Spirit's task to convict one of sin (John 16:8).

This is a mysterious process, the working of which is known only to God. In His interview with Nicodemus, Jesus compares the Holy Spirit's work to the wind. It is an invisible process. The wind blows, but it cannot be seen. The effects of the wind of the Spirit, however, are visible in the life of the individual in whom He works.

Because God is omnipotent, literally everything and everyone in all the world is at God's disposal for use in convicting sinners. The ways God uses to convict sinners are as varied and unique as the individual with and in whom He is drawing to himself.

Conviction, then, is God's unique way of revealing to the awakened sinner all that lies deep within. The sinner, knowing he stands guilty before God, does not like what he sees.

So it seems that God, in His mercy, doesn't reveal too much too soon. Otherwise, the convicted sinner would be led into despair by the horror of the awful crimes he discovers he has committed against a holy God. Therefore, God patiently works His grace and love so as to produce the miracle of the new birth in that individual. In the alchemy of this marvelous process, which serves to win a penitent sinner to himself, He applies large measures of hope to the human heart, so that He turns sinners into seekers after truth. This process of conviction is important because He wants men and women who, from the heart, will worship only Him.

Through the years, I've had people say to me something like, "Would you pray for my son [or daughter, or husband] that they'll be saved?" That's an awfully big thing to pray, and I'm certain these people have not weighed their request. Other steps might be needed first. Let me explain why with an illustration.

A mother might come to me and say, "Will you pray for my daughter that she'll be married?" The girl (or the mother) might be awakened to a desire for marriage, but I feel I should be asking some questions. Is she going with someone? Does she even have any friends? Instead of praying that the daughter will be married, it might be wise to begin praying that she'll become pleasant enough to at least have a friend. When that happens, then she might be able to move on to another step.

In a similar way, when someone has become awakened, it is not wise to rush in with a "plan of salvation," which will only lead him to a premature assumption that he is a Christian. Our prayer should be that God will help us to use Scripture in such a way as to bring the individual to conviction.

If someone is to be brought under conviction, those of us who are Christians need to understand something about sin.

Are people in trouble spiritually because they

inherited some spiritual defect from their parents or grandparents? No. They are in trouble because when they reach the age of accountability they deliberately turn to their own way—they commit their will to the principle and practice of pleasing themselves as the end of their being. That is *sin*.

Here is the essence of sin: Mere man has determined he's going to defy the only One in the universe who is wise enough, big enough and good enough to govern and rule men's lives. Man has climbed onto the throne of his own heart—a place only God can be. And there he sits as a sinner, determined to do only what he wants to do. But all the while, he is utterly dependent upon God for his very life and breath.

Sin not only *is* a crime, as we concluded in the previous chapter, it is insanity—moral insanity. We've already seen that sin is treason—open rebellion—against a righteous government, and leads to anarchy, where the only rule is: "I'm going to do what pleases me!" Because the law of God stands between man and his selfish appetites, the result of anarchic self-government is transgression of God's Law. God's Law is overthrown—but because it cannot be erased or destroyed, we stand guilty. To *understand* this is to come to true conviction.

Now the astounding thing is that after all of these crimes against God, you would think that He would be the sinner's enemy. But Scripture says that "the carnal mind is enmity against God"

(Romans 8:7). In other words, sinners have committed all these crimes against God, but it is the sinner who turns out to be God's enemy. And that's *why* we must be convicted of sin.

When I was in training for the ministry in Minneapolis, I visited prisoners. I gathered from the people on the other side of those bars that, at least in Minnesota, the miscarriage of justice was almost one hundred percent. Only once did I meet someone who was *justly* imprisoned.

"Why are you here?" I asked the fellow.

"Because the court was merciful to me," he said. "In fact, I should have been killed for my crimes. But I'm here on a life sentence. And I deserve to be here."

All the rest of the people I talked to who had been sentenced to imprisonment, in their own minds, were wrongly convicted.

Now we come to the question: *What* is conviction of sin? It is that state of the mind and heart when the individual takes sides with God against himself.

On this point, Scripture is clear: "All have sinned and come short of the glory of God" (Romans 3:23). Conviction is the work of the Spirit of God in the human heart that causes the individual to realize something of the enormity of the crime that he has committed against God.

The Bible holds an illustration of the wonderful thing that happens in the lives of those who side with God against themselves.

When Joseph had been in Egypt for a number of years, a band of rag-tag, footsore and hungry men from the land of Canaan came to him, begging for provisions to help their families survive the famine at home. Because Joseph had been away from them a long time—and because they supposed him dead—his brothers did not recognize him at all. But he knew them at once. And more than that, Joseph remembered the dream the Lord had given him years before—that his brothers would one day bow down to him. And now, here they were, crouched at his feet.

But the real question which Joseph needed to settle was this: Were their hearts changed? Had they ever been convicted of the heinous crime of selling their brother into slavery and then lying to cover their sin. It's possible, considering the evil capacity of the human heart, that they had even come to believe their own lies.

So to test them, Joseph accused them of being spies. Then he ordered them to prove they were honest men by returning home to bring back their youngest brother. Now they were up against it!

What was their response? "And they said one to another, We are verily guilty concerning our brother, in that we saw the anguish of his soul, when he besought us, and we would not hear; therefore is this distress come upon us ' " (Genesis 42:21).

They were convicted, not only of their sin, but of the fact that they deserved to be punished for what they had done. They had, at last, taken sides with God against themselves. "We are guilty." That is *accepting* conviction.

We find another example of godly conviction in Numbers 21:7:

> Therefore the people came to Moses, and said, We have sinned, for we have spoken against the Lord, and against thee; pray unto the Lord, that he take away the serpents from us. And Moses prayed for the people.

God has given us these testimonies that we might understand: We deserve judgment.

Now this gives many "New Testament Christians" a problem. "Don't talk about judgment. Talk about grace." In fact, I once heard a preacher say, "*Never* preach the Law. God is love. Just talk to sinners about the love of God. Everybody knows they've sinned."

If that is true, then how is it that we read: "Therefore by the deeds of the law there shall no flesh be justified in [God's] sight: for by the law is the knowledge of sin"? (Romans 3:20). And what about this statement: "Wherefore the law was our schoolmaster to bring us unto Christ, that we might be justified by faith" (Galatians 3:24).

None of us can give up the Word of God to

accept the metaphysics of certain preachers who think that God's holiness is a mere blemish on His escutcheon. God does not wear His holiness as an emblem to mark His sovereignty or as merely to identify himself. But there are preachers who pick and choose from the Word whatever will fit their dogma, thus passing on to their followers their own distortions. "By the law is the knowledge of sin," declares the Bible, and that Law has been written in the fabric of nature (see Psalm 19; Romans 1) and even in our own hearts.

When my wife and I went to Africa as missionaries a number of years ago, we'd had the customary training one receives in a fine Bible school. So we did not have high expectations about people who had never seen a missionary or heard the name of Jesus. As I prepared to travel into the bush to the Ganza tribe along the Sudan near the Ethiopian border, I was told that I was to be the first man ever to go to them with the Bible and the name of Jesus.

When I reached them, however, I found that these people knew an amazing amount—far more than I had been led to expect. For instance, all you had to do was break off a stick or pick up a stone and ask, "Who made this?" They would respond, "Wannamish." (God.) They also knew God was holy, and that He was angry with them because of their sin. They knew, too, about Satan— that he was evil. So they sacrificed chickens to him. This puzzled me.

"Why don't you bring your chickens to Wannamish, since He is good?" I asked.

"We don't know that he wants our chickens," they responded. "And we can't waste them on him if we don't know if he wants them. We know that if we do not take our chickens to evil spirits our goats will die and our crops won't grow. So we save all the chickens we can for the ones who want them—for the evil spirits."

The natives knew who God was, they knew He was angry with them when they did something wrong, and they knew He was going to punish them when they died. But there was no fear of God before their eyes. They were so interested in how to survive the harvest that they could not be particularly concerned about what was going to happen when they died.

"What have you done to make God angry with you?" I asked one of them.

"We've lied."

"What else?"

"We've stolen."

"Have you ever killed anyone?" I asked.

He hesitated. "Are you with the government?"

"No, I'm here to study your language and to talk with you about Jesus."

"Well, yes, I've killed. But. . ."

And then he began accusing others in the

tribe. He obviously did not want to be all alone in his crime.

So you see, the people of Africa instinctively knew the Ten Commandments. They knew it was wrong to lie, steal and kill. Who taught them? They had never seen a Bible. They had never heard the name of Jesus. No one had ever introduced them to the law of God.

Indeed, "when Gentiles" (Paul is talking about pagans—the kind of people I talked to in Africa), "who have not the law do by nature what the law requires, they are a law to themselves" (Romans 2:14).

There it is! Every member of the human family who comes off the assembly line, everyone who has ever been born of human parents comes with standard equipment: "the law written on their hearts."

In the book *Gospel Themes*, a collection of sermons preached by the late revivalist Charles G. Finney, he talks about "the inner revelation and the outer revelation." As an illustration, he used something appropriate to his day—the flour mills.

A flour mill was situated by a waterwheel, which had a lower stone moving in one direction, and an upper stone turning in the opposite direction. Finney said, "The outer revelation" of the Law, which comes to us through the written Word of God, is like the upper wheel. This bears down upon "the inner revelation," which is the inscribed knowledge of God and His Law written on the human heart. Thus our soul is caught between the millstones and ground fine, even as wheat is made into wholesome flour.

In the grinding process, the hull of the grain is taken off. We could say that the individual's sophistication is removed when he is brought under conviction of sin.

To me this is an excellent illustration of the use of God's Word in bringing the revelation of God's holiness and His Law down upon a man or woman anywhere in the world. And we know that the Spirit of God will cause hearts to be prepared for grace.

I want you to note one further thing which Finney's illustration so aptly reveals: Unless the upper millstone begins to turn, it merely rests on the lower millstone. There's no abrasion, no pressure, no friction. Thus the individual is content in his sin. But when the Word of God is brought to bear on the human spirit, a man must begin to examine his conduct, because the grinding has begun. For as scripture says, "by the law is the knowledge of sin." The Law of God causes us to see the true nature of sin—how exceedingly evil sin is, since it is a transgression against a Holy God.

It is imperative for us, therefore, to understand that God has not changed—nor has His Law. It is still His millstone, which He uses to cause the human ego to undergo this work of being shredded, ripped, crushed and pulverized.

Earlier, we looked at verses having to do with *awakening*. Now, let's examine verses for those who have been awakened, but who *are not yet under conviction*.

One place to start is with the Ten Commandments. It is wise to go back and refresh your memory; you'll be astonished at the way the Spirit of God reveals the holiness of the Father, Son and Holy Spirit through the Ten Commandments.

The Law, of course, is not restricted to the Ten Commandments. Everything that indicates the holiness of God has the effect of unveiling the heart. Keep in mind that it is the Holy Spirit who convicts. We do not know *how* He convicts of sin, but the effects are visible. Some of the effects, when the law is applied to the human conscience are these: unrest, distress, concern, unhappiness. The convicted individual says, "Something's the matter! I don't get any pleasure out of this thing anymore."

Unrest gives way to a burden—something psychologists broadly label "depression." But *conviction* is a burden on the mind and on the *spirit*. So when some people who are depressed try to escape from it, they find they cannot. For many, in reality, it is because the Spirit of God is dealing with them about their sin.

For instance, David talked about his "misery"

in Psalm 51. He cried, "My sin is ever before me." He had God's misery in his heart.

In Acts 2:37, it says: "They [the people] were pricked in their heart" when they heard the apostles' preaching because they felt conviction.

Probably one of the best scriptural examples of a convicted person is that of the publican who went down to the temple. He stood there in front of the veil of the temple with downcast eyes and beat his breast. While the Pharisee at his side was saying, "Thank God, I'm not like that fellow," the publican cried out to God: "Be merciful to me a sinner." (See Luke 18:9–14.)

On the other side of the veil, from where that convicted sinner stood, was the mercy seat—the place where blood was taken once a year by the high priest. The publican was in the right place and in the right attitude. He had taken sides with God against himself.

Conviction is not an intellectual agreement with the plan of salvation—it strikes deep, resounding chords of sorrow in the soul. God has a reason for saying that the Holy Spirit will convict of sin. His purpose is not just to give us a hell-insurance policy. He wants to save us from our sins. But until we discover what our sins are, we are not candidates to be saved from them.

I once asked a group of people at an evangelistic meeting, "How many of you are saved?" I'd say more than ninety percent raised their hands.

I was astounded. They'd hardly brought any unsaved persons into that meeting. They had planned the evangelistic meeting but, apparently, were not able to convince one unsaved person to attend.

Then I asked another question. "How many of you have ever been lost?" I don't believe I had ever asked that sequence of questions before. Four hands went up. Finally, I asked: "How in the world can you be saved if you've never been lost? Because the only kind of people God saves are *lost* people."

Quoting Matthew 18:11, I said, " 'For the Son of man is come to save that which was lost.' Is it possible only four of you can ever remember being lost? How is it then that all the rest of you are claiming to be saved? Either the Word of God is wrong, or all of you are suffering memory failure, because something isn't coming out the way it ought to."

Now for those of you who are Christians, it shouldn't be too difficult for you to remember when you were lost. It certainly isn't hard for me.

When I was about thirteen years old, I went to a two-week camp meeting—the old Red Rock meeting in South St. Paul, Minnesota. A certain girl was going to be there, and I wanted to be where she was.

Those two weeks of camp seemed to me to be a pretty good vacation—but I also had to attend services three times a day—morning, afternoon and evening. To attend, I also had to wear a cheviot suit. (If you don't know what kind of material cheviot is, I believe it consists of horse hair and barbed wire!)

I had to sit at those meetings in my suit, and I assure you I never fell asleep. In fact, I hardly sat down. Usually, I was positioned about half an inch off the seat.

Now, I was a good-standing church member. Until I attended those meetings, I felt I was all right. But about Friday or Saturday of that first week, I reached the conclusion that there were two kinds of Christians—the kind they were talking about and the kind *I* was. And on Sunday night, I realized I was not saved. But, of course, I could never tell anyone, because my mother thought I was a Christian. She would have been terribly disappointed if she found out I was not. So from Sunday to Wednesday night, I didn't get much sleep. I knew I was lost. I knew that if God did not have a hell He would have to make one when I died, because if I went to heaven the way I was I'd ruin the place.

That evening, the speaker preached a glorious exaltation of Christ. And afterward we were singing, "Just as I am without one plea. . . ."

Then the preacher said, "For the last three nights, I have not been able to sleep. I've been waking up in the middle of the night because I'm praying for someone who came on these grounds thinking he was saved and has found out he's lost.

"I don't know who it is, but as I prayed it seems to me I've seen in my mind a boy—about twelve or thirteen years old. I thought he was here in this place. Or maybe he's somewhere else. Now friends, you look down your aisle, and if you see somebody holding on to the bench in front of him that's probably who it is."

Well, I instantly dropped my hands from that bench, because as I looked around me I saw I was the only one who was holding on! When they sang the next verse of the hymn, "Just as I am," I headed for the altar, which was already full. Everybody else was with a counselor at the altar. But there I knelt, all the way at the end of the altar and I heard someone say, "Won't someone go to that boy over there?"

A man approached me. "What did you come for?" he asked.

"To be saved," I said.

"From what?"

"I didn't know I had a choice," I answered. "I want to be saved from sin." I was so lost. But that night I learned how I must be saved.

I believe people never come to the assurance of forgiveness until they are lost. Because no one can be forgiven as long as he justifies himself. Self-justification—the tendency to call a *wrong* thing *right* is always strong. It is an ancient bent in human nature.

We have only to journey back to the Garden of Eden and listen to how the first couple explained to God why they did not obey Him about eating from the forbidden tree.

In a mysterious way, not explained to us, Scripture says "they heard the *voice* of the Lord God *walking* in the garden in the cool of the day" (Genesis 3:8). Sadly, we find this couple, who once walked and talked daily with God their Creator, now hiding from His presence. And while the omniscient One knew exactly where Adam was, He allowed the man to describe his location and condition.

"I heard your voice in the garden, and I was afraid because I was naked; so I hid," said Adam.

"Who told you that you were naked? Have you eaten from the tree that I commanded you not to eat from?"

And Adam said, "The woman you put here with me—she gave me some fruit from the tree, and I ate it."

Do you see what's happening here? Adam readily justified himself, and put the blame on *God* for giving him a woman like Eve!

God turned to Eve and interrogated her: "What is this that you have done?"

And what does Eve do? She, too, passes on the blame! "The serpent deceived me, and I ate."

In the end, the pair was shut out of the Garden

of Eden. Ever since that moment in time, humanity has borne traces of this awful, spiritual disease—*sin*.

Now, we cannot justify ourselves. But because the Lord Jesus became our sin at Calvary, every sinner who chooses to be forgiven can be justified by faith and have peace with God. The Word of God tells us, "But God commendeth his love toward us, in that, while we were yet sinners, Christ died for us" (Romans 5:8).

The way of peace is open for the one who wants to be saved from sin. There's still time to obey God, as He is calling sinners to himself through Jesus Christ, the Son of His love.

Now we find, in evangelical circles today, a variety of popular teachers who espouse programs based on a "love" gospel, which is not the gospel of the Lord Jesus Christ. We must be aware that we need to train our spiritual senses to detect the false from the true workers in the Church. Through reading the Word of God, through prayer and through fellowship with mature Christians we are able to train our eyes to see clearly.

The world around us is full of strange voices. Jesus says, "My sheep know *My voice*." And His voice is unmistakably clear to the one who has his ears attuned to what is of God. This is why Jesus emphasized, "He that hath ears to hear, let him hear" (Matthew 11:15).

In *The Gospel According to Jesus*, MacArthur writes:

> True believers will persevere. If a person turns against Christ, it is proof that person was never saved. As the Apostle John wrote: "They went out from us, but they were not of us; for if they had been of us, they would no doubt have continued with us: but they went out, that it might be made manifest that they were not all of us" (1 John 2:19). No matter how convincing a person's testimony might seem, once he becomes apostate he has demonstrated irrefutably that he was never saved.

The true Christian is uncomfortable in surroundings that are not in harmony with heavenly things. The psalmist declares, "How shall we sing the Lord's song in a strange land?" (Psalm 137:4).

For those being held captive by workers who have ensnared them in their "love" programs, we see them portrayed in Psalm 137, weeping beside the rivers of Babylon. They're lost.

But even now the Good Shepherd hears their cry and is working out His plan to set them free. If their heart is toward the Lord, He will show them His salvation.

Conviction:

1. What does it mean when a sinner is convicted?
2. Why does a sinner need to be convicted? What is he convicted of?
3. Who brings conviction upon the sinner? What is His instrument of conviction?

Depth of Mercy

I have long withstood His grace,
Long provoked Him to His face,
Would not hearken to His calls,
Grieved Him by a thousand falls.
Now incline me to repent,
Let me now my sins lament;
Now my foul revolt deplore,
Weep, believe, and sin no more.

—Charles Wesley

FOUR

Repentance:

Making a 180-Degree Turn

For though I made you sorry with a letter, I do not repent, though I did repent: for I perceive that the same epistle hath made you sorry, though it were but for a season. Now I rejoice, not that ye were made sorry, but that ye sorrowed to repentance: for ye were made sorry after a godly manner, that ye might receive damage by us in nothing. For godly sorrow worketh repentance to salvation not to be repented of: but the sorrow of the world worketh death (2 Corinthians 7:8–10).

The lost condition leads into a state we call *repentance*. Throughout the Old Testament, prophets like Ezekiel, Hosea and Joel commanded repentance. And John the Baptist preached it in the New Testament. (See Luke 13:3–5.) "Except ye repent, ye shall all likewise perish."

Many preachers talk and write about repentance—however, we find an awful lot of nonsense about it. The way they handle it, you'd think that repentance means "being sorry for sin." I've even heard many preachers say, "You've got to be sorry enough about sin to quit."

The Greek word for repentance, I'm told, means "to change one's mind." That is, to change one's mind from one type of thinking to another.

A. W. Tozer writes:

> The Holy Spirit operates in another realm altogether, and the method of winning a man to God is a divine method, not a human one. Oh, we can make church members. We can get people over on our side, and they can join our class and go to summer camps. We may have done nothing but make proselytes out of them. When the Holy Spirit works in a man, then God does the work, and what God does, according to Scriptures, is forever.

MacArthur has this to say on the subject:

> Repentance has always been the foundation of the biblical call to salvation. When Peter gave the gospel invitation at Pentecost, in the first public evangelism of the church era, repentance was at the heart of it. "Repent and be baptized, every one of you, in the name of Jesus Christ for the forgiveness of your sins" (Acts 2:38). No evangelism that omits the message of repentance can properly be called the

gospel, for sinners cannot come to Jesus Christ apart from a radical change of heart, mind, and will. That demands a spiritual crisis leading to a complete turnaround and ultimately a wholesale transformation. It is the only kind of conversion Scripture recognizes.

Now, remember, sin is a crime. It is the committal of the will to the principle and practice of governing one's life to please one's self. In other words, when the Scripture says, "all have sinned," it is saying that upon reaching the age of accountability, every individual has chosen to govern and control his life to please himself.

Churches get into an awful lot of trouble when their leaders try to answer questions the Bible never answers. The Bible does not tell us *why* everyone sins. It just tells us *that* everyone sins. The moment you try to go beyond the Scripture, you enter into metaphysics or philosophy. We would do well to stay in the Scriptures. We know that upon reaching the age of accountability, each of us chose as the principle by which we would live: "I am going to govern and control my own life."

Some individuals are far more refined and cultured than others. They don't shake their fists in the face of God and say, "I'm going to do what I want to do." But whether they are *up* and out or *down* and out, the fact is Scripture says they're *out*. "All have sinned and come short of the glory of God." Whether they turned away with gritted teeth and jaw set—or whether they did it in a nice, sweet way—they still turned from Him. They have sinned. Either one is an equally treasonous crime.

When I was in Bible School I was taught *dispensationalism*. We were told that "repentance" has nothing to do with the "Age of Grace," that repentance was for the Jews. Now, friends, let me say this: Dispensationalism is like pregnancy. There is no such thing as a little bit of it. Once you get it, you will grow. It will fill you. And dispensationalism sure took hold of me.

Tozer says, "God will take nine steps toward us, but He will not take the tenth. He will *incline* us to repent, but He cannot do our repenting for us."

A friend once said to me, "Brother, I think there is something to this thing about repentance."

I quickly retorted, "Whatever you do, don't try to get me mixed up in that! Repentance is Jewish. It has nothing to do with us. We live in the Age of Grace."

Remarkably, it was another dispensationalist who set me straight. Harry A. Ironside who, at that time, was the pastor of Moody Church in Chicago startled his colleagues when he wrote his book, *Except Ye Repent*. He said:

> I think I'll break with my dispensationalist friends who try to tell me and others that re-

pentance is not for today. Because the Scripture makes it clear Paul said that he was in Ephesus night and day among the Jews and Gentiles preaching "repentance toward God and faith toward the Lord Jesus Christ."

You see, dispensationalists took the Law of God away from preparing hearts for conviction and repentance. I believe that, in doing so, they committed a greater crime against the Son of God than all of the "modernist" enemies put together. For they succeeded in disarming the Holy Spirit of the only instrument He ever provided himself to prepare men for grace.

Men must be convicted of sin. We must repent. Jesus Christ said, "Unless you repent, you will perish."

What, then, does it mean to repent?

Repentance means making a 180-degree turn. It means changing your mindset from "I'm going to do what *I* want to do," to, "Lord, I'm going to please *You* as long as I live." It is a change of mind, a change of intention, a change of purpose, a change of practice.

Repentance, it must be stated, doesn't earn us anything. A man is not doing any works. All he is doing, when he repents, is to realize the enormity of his crime in living to please himself and to gratify his appetites. He's not striking a deal with God. He's not trying to make any kind of bargain. He is simply saying, "From today on, I will change the purpose of my life. Now I will live to please God."

Spurgeon once said, "One repents because one has discovered that God deserves to be obeyed and served. It has to be voluntary—not induced or coerced. It has to be something the person does because he wants to do it and because God deserves it. Indeed, God deserves to be obeyed and served. Repentance, to be real, has to be hearty and not reluctant."

He added that if a person had a thousand sins and repented of only 999, there is no real repentance. You are merely trying to strike a bargain with God.

So we see that repentance has to be complete and not partial. Repentance is a committal of the will to the principle and practice of pleasing God in everything. That means, from today on, the Lord is going to be king and boss and sovereign. You do as He tells you. Because, out of love, He deserves to be obeyed and served. We need to understand this ourselves in order to proclaim it to others.

I would like to pose some questions. Have you ever been lost? Have you ever discovered your lostness? Have you known the enormity of your crime against God? Have you repented—that is, changed your mind about who's going to be boss? Have you purposed in your heart to please God in everything?

This is the nature of repentance. It is a change of mind—a change of intention—a change of purpose. It is not merely "accepting Christ."

"The whole 'Accept Christ' attitude is likely to be wrong," says Tozer. "It makes Him stand hat-in-hand awaiting our verdict on Him, instead of our kneeling with troubled hearts awaiting His verdict on us. It may even permit us to accept Christ by an impulse of mind or emotions, painlessly, at no loss to our ego and no inconvenience to our usual way of life."

It's possible, having just "accepted Christ," to say, "Well, I did that once. But some things have come along and. . . ."

Friend, if repentance is past-tense for you it's time you brought everything up-to-date. For without repentance you cannot begin to know God's so great salvation.

On the subject of repentance, Charles Finney said:

> Repentance always implies hatred of sin. It is feeling toward sin exactly as God feels. It always implies forsaking sin. Make sinners understand this! Repentant sinners don't feel what *un*repentant sinners think they do. Unrepentant sinners think if they become Christians, they will have to stay away from parties, theaters, gambling, or other things they now delight in. They think they would never enjoy themselves if they broke with those things.

But this is far from correct. Christianity doesn't make them unhappy by shutting them out from delightful things, because the first step in being a Christian is repentance, changing their mind about these things. They don't seem to realize that the repentant person has no longer any desire for those things; he has abandoned them, turned his mind from them.

Perhaps the Spirit of God has spoken to you about some area in your life that must change. Of course, it would have been wise to have dealt with it at the very moment God chose you. But the invitation is extended to you even today, and the invitation is this: If you are willing to confess every sin—if you believe that what you confess, He forgives—if you're willing to absolutely surrender everything to His will, then *believe it*. For what you have surrendered, He will receive. Talk to Him; pray to Him; make Him your Lord.

Perhaps you've heard people say, "I accepted Jesus as Savior six years ago. This year, at a summer conference, I accepted Jesus as Lord."

That simply is not biblical. The Word says, "If you will confess with your mouth the Lord Jesus. . . ." Literally, it is, "If you accept Jesus as Lord." That means allowing Him to be Lord in all things *today*.

At any point in your Christian pilgrimage, when you discover that your mind is not in accord with His mind, the issue has to be settled immediately. We don't fight it. Go right on changing your mind, conforming to His mind, as He reveals it.

Perhaps you have come across the tract *I Saw the Lake of Fire* being circulated by an evangelical group in North Carolina. It's the testimony of Charles McCormick who was a member of a group that preaches a false doctrine about the Lord Jesus Christ.

McCormick's family members were zealous witnesses and would go from house to house, leaving literature. He said they never had a Bible in his home, but they had stacks of printed material. As a young boy, he believed everything he read in the books his father promoted.

By the time he was twenty-one years old, however, he had moved away from his family. He had planned to go to a bookstore sponsored by the sect to which his family belonged. But before he could get there he had a dream:

> I dreamed that I was standing near the edge of a great plain. I began to feel very strange and uneasy. A company of people was passing by. Then I noted that some of them were carrying banners bearing the name of the religious organizations which they had founded or represented. Others could be identified by their dress. On the back of their garments there was a sign, "False Prophets." One of these men, who represented the religion I was trusting in, looked at me and said to the other false prophets, "There is one of my fol-

lowers." I looked in the direction which these men were traveling, and there in the distance I saw the lake of fire.

I make no attempt to describe that scene. In my dream, only one glimpse of this lake of fire caused me to fall to the ground, limp, overcome with fear and with the wrath of God. All I could do was to faintly wail, "Oh, God! I've followed a false prophet, and now it's too late. . . ."

McCormick said he did not know how to pray. But he said that during the days that followed, he had a great fear of God and the judgment.

Then he remembered some people who professed to be born again. They claimed that God had personally revealed to them that their sins had been forgiven. He writes:

One evening I attended a little mission where some of these people worshiped. As I sat through the service I began to feel a very heavy burden of sin on my heart. I decided to go straight to my apartment and pray all night, or pray until God revealed to me that my sins were forgiven. But the very instant I purposed to do this, that heavy burden left. God forgave me while I walked along the street toward my apartment. Great joy filled my heart. I experienced the wonderful salvation that was made available through the suffering and death of the Lord Jesus. I was free from all my old habits. I had no desire to run with the old gang or to attend the places where I had previously sought entertainment. I had experienced the new birth.

No one ordered Charles McCormick to do so, but he began reading the Bible every day and praying. He said that as he carefully studied the Scriptures he plainly saw that there was more for him in the way of God's great salvation.

In short, he had finally discovered a living faith—not just the *hope* of an afterlife. This type of faith is the next step we must make as we move deeper into God and the life He plans for us.

Repentance:

1. What is the essence of repentance?
2. Why is it necessary?
3. Is repentance still necessary today?

Trust and Obey

When we walk with the Lord
In the light of His Word,
What a glory He sheds on our way!
While we do His good will
He abides with us still,
And with all who will trust and obey.
Trust and obey—
For there's no other way
To be happy in Jesus
But to trust and obey.

—John H. Sammis

FIVE

Faith:

Seeing With Your Soul

Now faith is the substance of things hoped for, the evidence of things not seen. For by it the elders obtained a good report. By faith we understand that the worlds were framed by the word of God, so that things which are seen were not made of things which do appear. By faith Abel offered unto God a more excellent sacrifice than Cain, by which he obtained witness that he was righteous. . . . But without faith it is impossible to please him: for he that cometh to God must believe that he is, and that he is a rewarder of them that diligently seek him (Hebrews 11:1–6).

Hebrews offers us the only definition of faith in Scripture. I define it this way: Faith is the sight of the soul. It is the eyes of the human spirit, the ability to see what is not there yet—to see what's going to be there. That is something of an oversimplification, for there are deeper dimensions to faith that we must explore.

In his book *Revival Praying*, Leonard Ravenhill sums up faith in a way that is all-encompassing. He writes, "Through the channel of faith comes all that we have or ever will have in the Christian life this side of eternity."

"Faith is *super-sensory*," he adds. "It does not cling to logic; it does not have to abide by logic; it does not have to fear to be judged by logic."

God chose to illustrate the meaning of faith by involving Isaac. God told Abraham he was to take Isaac, his only son, down to the place that He would show him—and it was the place of sacrifice, Mount Moriah, where the temple was later to be built. God said, "Take Isaac down there and offer him to the Lord."

Now Abraham was a man of faith and he obeyed. Faith and obedience always are the same thing—two sides of the same coin.

It's interesting to note that Abraham could have gone from where they were to Mount Moriah, perform the sacrifice, and return the same day.

But God never told him *how* to get there, so Abraham went a little bit to the east—about a day's journey. Then he went a little bit southwest—another day's journey. I'm certain he wanted time with his young son, because he loved him. So he made the trip a little bit longer than necessary, and God did not scold him for that. God knew his heart.

When they were at the foot of the mountain, Abraham knew exactly what he had to do. He had to go up the mountain, put stones together, gather some wood, and have his son lie down on it. Then he had to raise the knife, slay his son and set the wood afire. He knew what sacrifice was. But listen to Abraham's faith. To his servant he said, "Abide ye here . . . and [*we* will] come again to you" (Genesis 22:5).

Abraham had resurrection faith! He said, "I'll do this. But God has promised He would bring me a seed from this lad. And if God wants Isaac, well and good. He gave him to me in the first place. He'll give him back to me again." That's faith!

Faith says, God is able to do what He has promised. God promised He would give Abraham a seed through Isaac, and He was there to perform what He had promised.

Romans 4 gives us a little more insight into what God wants Abraham's faith to mean to us. Verse 3 says: "For what saith the scripture? Abraham believed God, and it was counted unto him for righteousness." And then in verses 8–9 we read: "Blessed is the man to whom the Lord will not impute sin. Cometh this blessedness then upon the circumcision only, or upon the uncircumcision also? for we say that faith was reckoned to Abraham for righteousness."

Why is Abraham's faith important to us? Because it is this kind of faith that must be exercised to bring us into a saving relationship with Jesus Christ. Also, the promise God made to Abraham—that he would be the father of many nations—was not only to Abraham and the seed of his body, but to everyone who savingly embraces God's dear Son—the gift of His love. In other words, everyone born into the family of God through faith in Christ receives the promise of salvation.

With that in mind, we can better understand Acts 1:8, which says: "... after that the Holy Ghost is come upon you: and ye shall be witnesses unto me both in Jerusalem, and in all Judaea, and in Samaria, and unto the uttermost part of the earth."

We're talking about a faith that not only savingly unites us to Christ, but brings us into a relationship where the promise that was made to Abraham long ago can be fulfilled now—today—in those who believe in Jesus Christ.

MacArthur writes:

> This is Jesus' description of true faith. It starts with humility and reaches fruition in obedience. The obedience true faith produces is more than external; it is an obedience that issues from the heart. That is what makes it greater than the righteousness of the scribes and Pharisees. Jesus characterizes true righteousness—the righteousness that is born of faith (Romans 10:6)—as obedience not just to

the letter of the law, but to the spirit of the law as well (Matthew 5:21–48). This kind of righteousness does not merely avoid acts of adultery; it goes so far as to avoid adulterous thoughts. It eschews hatred the same as murder. Jesus sums up the gauge of real righteousness in this shocking statement from the Sermon on the Mount: "Be perfect, therefore, as your heavenly Father is perfect" (Matthew 5:48).

During the years that God has privileged me to serve Him by preaching His Word, I've discovered several kinds of faith. They need to be clearly identified.

Head Faith: This is an intellectual assent to what is written in the Word. There are multitudes of people in the churches who think themselves to be born of God, because they intellectually or mentally have assented to what they read on the page. Multitudes of people think themselves to be right with God, but they have nothing more than the blueprint of a house which should have been built on the Rock.

The fact that you or I may agree that God's Word is true does not mean His Word is true *in* us. It is true on the page; but is it true *in* you? We need to distinguish between what our minds *perceive* and what our hearts have *received*. There's a great deal of difference.

It is my personal opinion (I do not make this a test of fellowship), that those who have an intellectual assent of the plan of salvation have never built their house on the Rock through the work of grace, which is this process: awakening, conviction and repentance. In the day of Judgment they will find their little house has been torn down by the flood of God's wrath. They gave an intellectual assent—a mental agreement to what is written. But that is not the faith we mean.

Dead Faith: This is equally devastating. I found "dead faith" among our Muslim friends when we were in the Sudan.

Sahid was our cook at the mission home in Khartoum. He came to us on Sunday evening to tell us he was starting out with a group of missionaries to drive across the desert about 3,500 miles to Lagos, in Nigeria. This is one of the hardest drives in the world. Sahid was going to cook for the missionaries, but he was also going to his home. He had left forty-four years earlier on a pilgrimage to Mecca, but now he was going back.

"I want to say 'goodbye' to you," he said to me. "I'm leaving."

"You've been a devoted man, Sahid."

"Yes, I've been to Mecca twice," he explained.

"Have you fasted every Ramadam?" I asked. That is Islam's holiest season.

"Oh yes, every Ramadam. Ever since I was a boy."

That meant that for a whole month, from sun-up until sun-down, Sahid never ate, or drank, or swallowed his spittle.

"Have you tithed?"

"Oh yes."

To the Muslim, tithing is not merely giving *ten percent* of what he earns, but each year tithing two percent of all that he possesses.

"Have you prayed, Sahid?"

"Oh yes! Five times a day."

"Sahid," I asked, "do you have peace in your heart? Do you know, if you died, that you would go to be with God?"

"Oh no! I don't have that. I can only hope that my good works may be such that, when I die, Mohammed will reach down and take my hand and help me across the abyss, so that I will not have to suffer."

Sahid observed rituals, rites, and taboos. There were things he could and could not do—things he could eat and not eat. He had observed them all. But his was a dead faith.

If I had asked, "Is Mohammed living in you?" Sahid would have laughed at me. His god, Mohammed, was buried. His ashes are there in the *Kaaba* of Mecca.

And if I had asked, "Does God ever reveal to you that you are His?" Sahid would have laughed again.

Friends, there are multitudes who name the name of Christ, and who are associated with Christian groups, but have accepted only rituals and taboos. They abstain from this and observe that. They have been baptized and catechized. But they are unaware that salvation is not a system of doctrines, taboos, or rituals.

They do not know that salvation means having the life of Christ in you. "He that has the Son has life." They have everything but Christ, and so they have a dead faith.

Devil's Faith: This is an emotional response to the horrors of hell and the beauties of heaven. It is the kind of faith that the demon expressed the day he cried out, "Have you come to judge us before the time?" He had faith that Jesus Christ was God—that He was going to be judged by Him. But he remained a devil. We read in James, "The devils believe and tremble." But they remain impenitent and are devils nonetheless. Their emotional response is: "I don't want to go to that horrible place. I like what I've heard about heaven. I want to go there, so I'll believe anything I need to believe, in order to escape the one place and gain the other." That is a devil's faith.

Heart Faith: In Romans 10, we discover a very distinct and definite statement—a delineation as to the kind of faith that savingly unites us to Jesus Christ:

But what does it say? "The word is near

you; is in your mouth and in your heart," that is, the word of faith we are proclaiming: But what saith it? The word is nigh thee, even in thy mouth, and in thy heart: that is, the word of faith, which we preach; that if thou shalt confess with thy mouth the Lord Jesus, and shalt believe in thine heart that God hath raised him from the dead, thou shalt be saved (Romans 10:8–9).

People can have an intellectual assent—they may appropriate doctrines and submit to rituals, but not know saving faith. Maybe you've even sung these words by Daniel Whittle:

> I know not how this saving faith to me He did impart, or how believing in His Word wrought peace within my heart.

"Saving faith, to me He did impart. . . ." Do you think for one moment that an impenitent wretch, trying to bargain with God, can stretch the arms of his spirit across 2,000 years past, see a Jew dying on a Roman jibbet and truly believe that the death of that Man could change his eternal destiny and his character, *without* help from God?

No, indeed. His faith must be made alive! And that is saving faith—or heart faith—in response to repentance.

That's why Paul said to the people of Ephesus: "And how I kept back nothing that was profitable unto you, but have shewed you, and have taught you publickly, and from house to house, testifying both to the Jews, and also to the Greeks, repentance toward God, and faith toward our Lord Jesus Christ. " (Acts 20:20–21).

It must be in that order. For in that way heart faith is released.

The word *believe* has been badly abused. It has gotten down to this: A little tip of the hat to what is written. That is what I call "head faith." But the word in the Anglo-Saxon, as the King James translators used it, was a good word.

What does it mean to *believe*? Believe literally means: to be; to exist; to live or have your being live in accordance with.

In medieval Britain, when a lord, a duke, or important nobleman who owned a vast estate was wounded in battle, he would assign one of his servants to fight until he had recovered. So the life of the nobleman was spared by his faithful servant.

In response to this kind of goodness and faithfulness, the nobleman would eventually give the servant his freedom. The man would be given a team of horses, some cattle, some chickens and ducks and a little place of his own. But because he was once related in service to the nobleman, he was still subject to call.

"If I ever need you, will you come to my aid?" the nobleman would ask his former servant.

"Oh yes, I'll come."

So it might happen a liveryman would appear one day at the door of the man's house, where he lived in tranquility and freedom with his wife and family.

"The nobleman needs you. Be at the castle tomorrow at dawn."

"What's the matter?"

"We're being threatened. You must bring your bow and arrows."

And so the man prepared for battle. His wife had no difficulty understanding the urgency of the call. They did not sleep that night. Very early in the morning, as the man prepared to depart, he looked down at his baby boy in the crib. He may never return. He has pledged his life to another. He says farewell to his family and his home and, in the early dawn, he leaves for the castle.

On the way, he meets other soldiers. They all gather in the courtyard and wait for daylight. At the rising of the sun, the door opens and a voice calls them to enter one by one.

Our man enters into the castle, where the nobleman greets him. "How are you, friend?"

"Fine, sir."

"Will you take my sovereign and bite into it?"

"Oh yes sir. I will, indeed."

Then an attendant comes and gives the man a gold coin belonging to the nobleman. The man bites deep into it. His toothprint is embedded in the soft gold coin, a mark every bit as good as his fingerprint. He bit into the nobleman's sovereign: His mark—his very name—is written on it.

To the nobleman, it means: This man believes on me. He will live and act in accordance to my rule, government and commands.

And that is the kind of believing faith that results ultimately in God's so great salvation.

To come to the Lord Jesus Christ is to commit ourselves to Him. It means we are going to live in accordance with His will as long as we live. We're going to bite into His sovereign, so to speak. We're going to commit all to Him, just as Abraham committed his all to God.

Are you that kind of believer? You are if you have been awakened, convicted, repented and now, by faith, want to be born into the family of God. Faith, as defined by the God of the Bible, means that we obey the wooing of His Spirit, that we willingly and obediently give ourselves to Him through Jesus Christ. That is saving faith, and it is the only kind of faith acceptable in God's sight.

Having given ourself to Him, that principle of giving must continue moment by moment. Everything the Christian is and has belongs to God. Keep this point clear: *A Christian is merely the custodian of what God has given him.*

Someone has said that no one has ever been able to give with greater return and with so little risk, than when he places himself and all that he has into the hands of God.

That is a simple description of the principle of "living by faith." Surely we can trust God to keep His Word. Then let us continue exercising what little faith we have, so that faith can grow deep in our hearts and be summoned to the surface when needed.

As God's new creation in Christ Jesus, His likeness must be reflected in the characteristics of our daily lives. We must bring God into every facet of our living and trust Him wholly. That's what it means to "live by faith."

Not only in the eyes of God, but in the eyes of the world, Christians are to be like Christ in their habits, their conversation, and in all the pursuits of life. Our part is to obey; God's part is to perform what He promised He would do according to His Word. God will never command us to do anything unless He comes with His own power to enable us to obey Him.

Living by faith is for every believer in Jesus Christ—for every area of one's life—not just for missionaries in the field, not just for preachers and evangelists.

The Christian life is a "walk" of faith. Step by step, day by day, we discover that the Lord is conforming us more and more to His will. He wants to mold and fashion us into His likeness, while working in us only as much as we are able to bear. His purpose is to make us vessels He can use for His glory.

Let us dare to open ourselves more and more to Him, so He may have freedom to work in us and through us. Only this way will we bring glory to our heavenly Father.

Faith:

1. What is a simple definition of faith? Faith cannot be separated from behavior. Why?
2. How do you go about turning "head faith"— or any of the other types of faith described in this chapter—into "heart faith"?
3. Christians talk about living or "walking" by faith. What does the "walk" of faith mean to you?

Ye Must Be Born Again

Ye children of men, attend to the word
So solemnly uttered by Jesus the Lord;
And let not this message to you be in vain,
"Ye must be born again."
O ye who would enter that glorious rest
And sing with the ransomed the song of the
    blest,
The life everlasting if ye would obtain,
"Ye must be born again."
"Ye must be born again,
Ye must be born again";
I verily, verily say unto thee,
"Ye must be born again."

—Wm. T. Sleeper

SIX

The New Birth:

The Blowing of the Wind

Except a man be born again, he cannot see the kingdom of God (John 3:3).

But as many as received him, to them gave he power to become the sons of God, even to them that believe on his name: Which were born, not of blood, nor of the will of the flesh, nor of the will of man, but of God. (John 1:12–13).

In response to heart faith a marvelous thing happens. In heaven, we are justified: The record against us has changed; that is to say, our standing before God has changed.

Justified means it is as though I had never sinned. Our sins have been laid on Christ. They were accounted to Him. We have been forgiven, pardoned. Our sins have been washed away, never again to be held against us. It is a legal matter, decided eternally once and for all.

In our hearts, we were *born again* when we believed! God, the Holy Spirit, has quickened us. Our spirit has been joined to Him by that life-giving touch. We become, as it were, new creations. He has restored contact with us who were once separated from Him by our sins.

Let me illustrate what it means to be "dead in sin."

Let's say you arise in the morning, turn on your television set to get the early news—and nothing comes on. There's no sound or picture. So you turn to your wife and say, "The TV is dead." Does that mean it is annihilated? Does it mean that during the night the TV set rusted out? Could you take a whisk broom and dust off the insides?

No, the TV set is there. Maybe a transistor is burned out. Maybe a wire is loose. But a connection is broken. The TV set has become separated from its source of power. Death always means separation.

Seeing that we were spiritually separated from Him, God made us with receiving sets, in order to know Him.

We live beneath three elements, or atmospheres, so to speak. The first atmosphere we live in is the ocean of *air*. In our body—or our receiving set—we have lungs. We get air to our lungs through our nostrils and through our mouth. If someone were to cover our mouth and pinch our nostrils, within a few moments we would be a statistic. In this atmosphere, we live and move. From it, we have our being. Air *must* be channeled into our receiving set.

The second atmosphere in which we live is that of sound. All around us are soundwaves. If we were to turn up all the electronic soundwaves to 100 decibels, buildings would be shattered. There is an ocean of electronic sound everywhere around us, but we need a receiving set to separate the sounds.

The third atmosphere in which we live is called *God*. On Mars Hill, Paul said, "For in him we live, and move, and have our being" (Acts 17:28). We have a receiving set to know God, and it is called "the human spirit." But as long as the human being who owns that spirit is living in rebellion against God—as long as he is a traitor and has never been convicted of his crime, if he has never repented of his crime and has never exercised faith—his receiving set is *dead*.

But when God, in His sweet grace and wonderful power, responds to the heart of faith we have mentioned earlier, the first thing He does is to repair the receiving set—that is, the human spirit.

The tragedy of today's "easy believism" is that the products of it do not get their assurance from God himself. And so many people say, "Oh, I've tried to be a Christian. It just doesn't work." It doesn't work because their broken connection never was repaired!

It has been reported that, in present-day evangelism, only one person out of two hundred first-time decisions for Christ continues to live as a Christian two years later. That is because many who made their decisions are products of human effort. When people leave the place of decision-making they are emotionally charged. Those converts usually go back to what they were before they made their decisions. In effect, they wash the whole thing off. Nothing is real.

But if an individual truly has been born of God—if God has repaired their receiving set—they learn from God himself that they are His child. That makes a big difference.

Tozer wrote in the book *When He Is Come*:

> So it is that the human being can know about God, he can know about Christ's dying for him, he can even write songs and books, be the head of religious organizations and hold important church offices and still never have come to a vital, personal knowledge of God at all. Only by the Holy Ghost can he know God.

In the early part of the nineteenth century—from 1837 to 1850—Charles Finney held meetings in upstate New York. God was blessing him. He incurred the wrath of the Presbyterians of his day though he was an accredited clergyman in their ranks. Finney had instituted what he called "the anxious seat." It was a section in the church reserved for those he termed "the anxious ones," the people who had been awakened, were under conviction of sin and were moving toward repentance. Those anxious ones were given a ticket on which their name was written. They would sit in the section of the church that had been reserved just for them.

When Finney was preaching in Albany, New York, the entire State Supreme Court attended the meetings. During a service, the Chief Justice of the New York State Supreme Court stood up.

Finney recognized him: "Mr. Finney," said the chief Justice, "you have carried your case. The evidence you've presented is convincing. If you are prepared to open the anxious seat, I am prepared to come forward."

During the course of that meeting, according to the records, every member of the New York State Supreme Court came to have a personal, experiential knowledge of the Lord Jesus Christ.

But because Charles Finney had established the anxious seat, he was ostracized by the Presbyterians and was then received by the Congregationalists, at the invitation of Henry Ward Beecher, of New York City. More trouble began when Henry's brother, Lyman, refused to have Finney be a part of the Congregational Church. (Incidentally, Lyman and Henry were brothers of Harriet Beecher Stowe, best remembered as the author of *Uncle Tom's Cabin*.) As the pastor of a

Congregationalist Church in Boston, Massachusetts, Lyman Beecher raised claims that the people who had come to Christ under Finney's preaching were not sound Christians.

But years later, Finney was in Rochester, New York, where a blue-ribbon committee of outstanding citizens was appointed by Henry Ward Beecher to study the converts who, a decade earlier, had come to Christ under Finney's preaching. It was found that eighty-five percent of those who had made professions of faith under Finney's preaching were still faithfully living for Christ!

In contrast, it is being reported that only one-half of one percent of those who make decisions for Christ in our evangelistic meetings today will be living as Christians two years from now. This should give you some idea of how far we've strayed from the Word of God.

I dare to say it: *No one in the universe has the right to tell a person he is born of God, except the Holy Spirit who is the spirit of adoption.* He has never relinquished that right to anyone. That is His sovereign prerogative.

On the subject of the new birth, our Lord Jesus Christ is the paramount authority. It was He who established once and for all the universal and indispensable need for the regeneration of individual souls.

More than 250 years ago, John Wesley was used of God in England to bring multitudes of people into a saving relationship with our Lord Jesus Christ. This great man left us some powerful sermons, which I have been reviewing recently. He asks the question, "What is the new birth?" His conclusion:

> The new birth is that great change which God works in the soul, when He brings it into life and raises it from the death of sin to the life of righteousness. The new birth is the change wrought in the soul by the almighty Spirit of God, when that soul is created anew in Christ Jesus. The Spirit renews the soul of man after the image of God and adds to it righteousness and true holiness.

Wesley often affirmed what our Lord said: "You must be born again." He wrote:

> So desperately wicked and so deceitful are the hearts of men that they flatter themselves by living in their sins until they come to their last breath. Thousands really believe they have found a way to live. But it is a broad way and will lead them to destruction.

We all know people who consider themselves to be so honest and of such strict morality that they cannot see how they can miss heaven. But when John Wesley encountered such people in his day he never failed to warn them of God's wrath against those who live a self-righteous life. The renowned preacher would say:

It may be that you are doing just as well as your unholy neighbors. But you, like them, will die in your sins. You shall drop into the pit together. All of you will lie together in the lake of fire—the fire that burns with brimstone.

Where do we hear such "fire and brimstone" messages today? Our evangelists talk in dulcet tones only of love, and the result is that people are won to themselves instead of to God. Can this be the reason we see so few honest decisions for Jesus Christ?

And we have little emphasis upon holiness in our evangelistic crusades today. John Wesley, on the other hand, thundered that no one can be holy until he is born again. He added that holiness is the prerequisite to knowing God's so great salvation.

"Without inward and outward holiness, you cannot be happy even in this world," said Wesley, "and much less will you be happy in the world to come."

We've all heard people say, "But I'm not harming anyone with my life. I'm honest. I don't curse. I don't take the Lord's name in vain. I'm not a drunkard. I . . ."

And then there are many who defend themselves like this: "I do the best I can with what I am. I do all the good I can for all the people I can."

Such a defense would not stand before a preacher like John Wesley. He wrote:

> You've had a thousand opportunities for doing good, and you have let them pass you by. Therefore, you are accountable to God for all the good you could have done, but that still would not change things. You must be Born Again. Because without New Birth, all the good you do does not help your poor, sinful, polluted soul.

Just as in Wesley's time, today we find many people hiding behind their good standing in the local church. They are the very pillars of the church. May God raise up faithful preachers, like John Wesley, who will dare to meet such people with hard words. Because in the reading of his sermons, I have been deeply moved by his faithfulness to God's Word.

> "Go to church twice a day," he wrote. "Go to the Lord's table every week. Say as many prayers in private as you can pray. And then listen to all the sermons you care to hear. Read all the books you can read about Christ. Still you must be Born Again."

Are we ready for preaching like this? Are you and I prepared to listen to preaching which, by the Spirit, pounds in our hearts? Are you willing to know the inward work of God in your life? For the one who will respond affirmatively to these questions, Wesley left a prayer that we all should make our own:

> Lord, add this to all thy blessings. Let me be Born Again. Deny me whatever pleases you, but don't deny me this. Let me be Born from Above. Take away whatever seems good to you. Take my reputation, my fortune, my friends, and my health. But give me the privilege of being Born of the Spirit. Let me be received among the children of God.

Is that your prayer? Do you truly desire to be born "not of corruptible seed, but of incorruptible" by the Word of God, which lives and abides forever?

We've been asked, What does it mean to be born again?

Jesus, in His interview with Nicodemus, presented only a few particulars and left no manuals to the scholarly Pharisee—or to us—on "how to be born again." So solemnly and uncompromisingly, our Lord said: "I tell you the truth, unless a man is born again [or "from above"], he cannot see the kingdom of God."

The Lord insists: If you are to be My disciple, you must be mine heart and soul—or you are not My disciple at all. We see that with the Lord Jesus, it is not a question of doing—or not doing—but of *being*.

Nicodemus was puzzled. "How can these things be?"

Jesus wanted Nicodemus to know that no man can predict the course or method of the New Birth. So as they sat together in the cool of the night, with a Galilean breeze wafting their brows, He used the wind to describe how the Spirit works *invisibly*, producing the inward grace of death to sin and a new birth unto righteousness.

Jesus went no further than a few simple remarks to give Nicodemus a glimpse of this mystery of the kingdom of heaven. It was a truth undreamed of, but now it was being fully revealed to this rich and scholarly man.

The night deepened about them. The conversation ended. But the work of God in the heart of Nicodemus continued. We hear from him in John 7, where we find him defending Jesus against the accusing Pharisees.

When the Pharisees accused the Lord of cursing the Law of Moses, Nicodemus said, "Does our law condemn a man without first hearing him to find out what he is doing?"

Then on the night Jesus died on the cross, it was Nicodemus who offered the spices, a hundred pounds worth, for embalming the dead body of Jesus. That act was a small but bold testimony of the inward work of the Spirit of God in the heart of the Pharisee who had first met Jesus on that Galilean night a good while before the crucifixion.

The New Birth is a mystery.

It is God alone who reveals His work of love and grace to the individual who is born into His kingdom. Only He can tell you when you are born again. But tell you He will.

For us to go beyond the teaching of the Lord in these matters, I believe, is like trying to tear apart a rose to discover its fragrance. We'd only be left with dead petals, while the beautiful rose would be gone forever. We must never go beyond what God has given in His Word about the mysteries of the kingdom of heaven.

Those who are truly born from above will continue to grow in grace and in the knowledge of our Lord and Savior Jesus Christ. In doing so, it is not possible for them to miss the further blessings of God's so great salvation, which we must now consider.

The New Birth:

1. What happens at the "new birth"?
2. Why is it necessary?
3. What are some evidences of the new birth?
4. Is it possible to be holy without it?

Spirit of Faith, Come Down

No man can truly say
That Jesus is the Lord,
Unless Thou take the veil away,
And breathe the living word.
Then, only then, we feel,
Our interest in His blood,
And cry with joy unspeakable:
Thou art my Lord, my God.
Inspire the living faith,
Which whosoe'er receives,
The witness in himself he hath,
And consciously believes.
The faith that conquers all,
And doth the mountain move,
And saves whoe'er on Jesus call,
And perfects them in love.

—Charles Wesley

SEVEN

The Witness of the Spirit:

You Tell Me After He Tells You

> But when the fullness of the time was come, God sent forth his Son, made of a woman, made under the law, to redeem them that were under the law, that we might receive the adoption of sons. And because ye are sons, God hath sent forth the Spirit of his Son into your hearts, crying, Abba, Father (Galatians 4:4–6).

When John Wesley began to preach in 1737, the churches of England closed their doors to him. Even at Epworth, where his father had been rector, he had to preach outside the church. He stood on his father's tomb and preached to the people of the village. The reason the churches had closed their doors to Wesley was because he said, "It is not enough to have your name on the church roll or to be baptized as an infant. It is not enough that you have been catechized, or that you have been taken into the church as an adult." John Wesley insisted you must have the witness of the Spirit to tell you that you are born of God.

At first, Wesley was hurt about not being permitted in the church. Then he realized that this was God's way of letting him get to the people.

From then on, Wesley would send someone into the community where he was planning a meeting that week. That "advance man," as it were, would tell the rectors of the local Anglican churches, "Wesley is coming." He would always have them ask the church leader if he could use their church to get the gospel message to the people.

There was always a negative response. In fact, the word was passed among the congregations: "Don't listen to Wesley."

The result of that kind of advertising, of course, was that the people came in droves to hear John Wesley.

I know something about the negative approach. When I was a boy in northern Minnesota, my mother would leave me to babysit my little brother. As she left she would say, "Now children, whatever you do, do not put pussy willows up your nose."

Mothers know how mischievous boys can be. Their youngsters are experts at doing things they are not supposed to do. Young boys are willing to attempt impossible things—especially when they're told they must *not* do them.

In our neighborhood, a mother had only recently suffered through having to call the doctor to her home to extract pussy willows from a little boy's nostrils. So before my mother left the house that day, she emphatically ordered us not to try what the neighbor's boy had done. To tell you the truth, we had never thought about doing it. But we could not wait until she was out of sight, because there had to be something wonderful about putting pussy willows up one's nose.

And so, (you guessed it!) the doctor had to be called to snare the pussy willows out of our noses.

Now you understand how God provided for Wesley. It is reported that one thousand people came to hear him. The rectors, though they didn't realize it, had gotten the people for him.

What did Wesley preach? *No one has the right to think themselves a child of God unless they have the witness of the Spirit to the new birth!*

Is that a feeling? Is it emotion? No! When someone would ask Wesley about this, he would quote Job: "But there is a spirit in man: and the inspiration of the Almighty giveth them understanding" (Job 32:8). And then he would quote: "For what man knoweth the things of a man, save the spirit of man which is in him?" (1 Corinthians 2:11).

The spirit is the part of you that knows you

are here and not somewhere else. It is the part of
you that knows you're married and not single, or
single and not married. It's the part of you that
knows you're a man and not a woman, or a
woman and not a man. It's the part of you that
God joins in the new birth—the part of you which,
as God quickens your heart in this new creation,
He tells you and you *alone*. Because then you
know that you know! That is what the witness of
the Spirit is.

I was speaking on this theme at an Inter-
Varsity alumni meeting in Cedar Point, Michigan.
When I finished, a woman named Harriet Marsh,
a staff member from New York City, was asked to
speak. She gave this testimony:

"Many of you know that my parents were not
Christians. But perhaps you did not know that my
father was an atheist and my mother was an agnostic—probably an atheist as well. I never attended church except for one funeral and a wedding until I attended college. At Douglas College,
the women's section of Rutgers University, I met
one young woman whose face was so radiant. And
her personality was utterly charming. I asked
some of the students about her, and learned she
was a believer—a Christian.

"The person in charge of assigning rooms at
the university was friendly with my parents. I
asked if I could room with that radiant young
woman when her roommate would leave in Jan-
uary. So I was given the privilege of moving into

that room and living close to that girl.

"I was with her only a short time. But in talking with her and listening to her speak and pray, a great hunger came into my heart. So I opened my heart to Christ. I went to prayer meetings and Bible studies. For me, it was an entirely new life.

"One of the professors at Rutgers, also an atheist, knew my father. From time to time, the professor took me out to lunch.

"Whenever we'd meet, he would say, 'You've got to give up this ridiculous nonsense. You're involved with religious superstition.' He'd work on me every time we met. 'You're too brilliant a student to waste your time with that stuff.'

"Finally, I succumbed. I told my roommate and friends at the Bible study group, 'You're nice people. I like being with you, but I have been deceived. I am not a Christian. It's just a mental and emotional thing with me, because you all are warm and understanding. I'm giving this all up today. I want your friendship, but please don't ever talk to me about the Bible or about Jesus.' "

Harriet said her Christian friends were disappointed, of course, but they agreed not to talk to her about the Bible or about Jesus. But, she had not said, "Do not pray for me."

Time passed. One day, as she was in the college library, she found herself praying the agnostic's prayer: "Oh God, if there is a God, save my soul, if I have a soul."

Later, she was in her room and remembered that her roommate would kneel to pray. "I'll do just this one last thing," she said. So she locked the door and fell to her knees. Again she said the agnostic's prayer.

Then she continued quietly to pray. From her heart and lips came these words, "Dear heavenly Father . . ." Instantly, it dawned on her what she had said. She began to laugh and cry. She unlocked the door and ran down the hall to where her friends were attending Bible Study.

"It's real! It's real! It's real!" she shouted. This time, Harriet *knew* she was born into the family of God.

Take another look at the opening text: "Because you are sons, God sent the Spirit of his Son into our hearts, the Spirit who calls out *Abba* Father."

Do you see it? Do you understand? Here is defined for us "faith," the "new birth," and "the witness of the Spirit." We must all come by this route, and if you have been brought by any other, this is the day to right your course.

Now, I want to make several very crucial observations relative to the witness of the Spirit.

The apostle John tells us, "And he that keepeth his commandments dwelleth in him, and he in him. And hereby we know that he abideth in us, by the Spirit which he hath given us" (1 John 3:24).

I dare to repeat unequivocally: *God the Holy Spirit is the only one who has the right to give you assurance that you are born from above.*

If we meet someone who says, "Well, I *hope* to go to heaven when I die." Or if they say, "I said the sinner's prayer one time, and I didn't feel anything at all," it is *not* our place to pour assurances into them. The fact that they doubt their salvation is enough for them to be fearful. We are doing them a grave disservice to give them a false hope.

The church world is teeming with people who are actively engaged in programs they believe are earning them salvation. But the sad truth is, they have no peace of God within. It is not our place to coddle or comfort these people. Rather, they need to be stirred into seeking after Christ as Lord and Savior.

Our Lord did offer the promise of comfort and assurance—but not to sinners. "Another Comforter," the Holy Spirit, He said would come to His followers—to those who would be like orphans—after He left the earth to go to the Father.

The sinner knows absolutely nothing about this. But when you know you have believed on the Lord Jesus Christ, when you know by the assurance He gives by His Spirit to your spirit that you are born again—then you may know beyond a shadow of a doubt that you are safe in Him. And then He will do all that is needed to protect and keep you in your new life.

Through His gracious work of regeneration, He seals us with the witness of His Spirit. He has brought us out of death into life. This is how we know that He is in us—"by the Spirit which He has given us."

Do you know that the gospel of John was written "that we might *have* eternal life"? And that the first epistle of John was written "that we might *know* that we have eternal life"? The earnest servant of God should be totally familiar with these important portions of Scripture.

In 1 John 5:6 it also says, "This is he that came by water and blood, even Jesus Christ; not by water only, but by water and blood. And it is the Spirit that beareth witness, because the Spirit is truth."

Someone told me recently that, as a student at Baptist College in New York State, his teacher said, "Now remember, it's your responsibility to let the Holy Spirit tell the one you're leading to Christ that he has been born of God." I am grateful that this is not some novel truth which I, personally, have "discovered," or which I'm trying to "sell." This is something that the Church has believed since the very beginning. The Holy Spirit is the spirit of adoption.

He is the only One who ever has been authorized to tell a human being that he has passed from death to life, that he has been brought out of darkness into life, that he has been born into the family of God, that he can call Almighty God, "*Abba, Father.*"

When I was a student in Bible School we used to have to report how many people we had won to the Lord in the previous week. Some of us got a little tired of not being able to report great successes.

So I went with a friend who taught me how to do it. We would take a handful of nickels to a bus stop and approach those who were there waiting for a bus. Then we'd say to them: "If you were to die today, would you go to heaven or to hell?"

"Oh, I don't know," most would respond.

"Would you like to know?"

"Oh yes."

"Well, it's a free gift," we'd say. "If you just accept Jesus Christ. . . ."

"What do you mean, it's a free gift?"

We'd hand that person a nickel and say, "Take it! In the same way you took my nickel, that's how you take Jesus Christ."

"Oh sure! All right!"

And we'd go on: "Now say this prayer after me . . ."

Thereafter, every Monday morning in chapel, we could report how many people *we* had won to the Lord. Of course, we should have been reporting how many nickels we gave out that week. But we would never want to get caught in that.

Until a transaction takes place between us and

the Spirit of God, there is no peace, no guidance from above, because the human spirit is dead to heavenly things. We are born of the Spirit only as the Spirit bears witness to our spirit that we are born of God. Life in God comes to every believer only in this way—though we may not even be aware of the process or know that there *is* a Holy Spirit! (See also Romans 8:16–17; 1 John 5:6.)

We must face the fact that there are two possible heresies. One is the heresy of the message. Usually we are all very well-equipped to detect that. But the other is the heresy of the method. That is the most subtle and most dangerous of heresies.

Many times the message preached is orthodox, but the method is mixed with error. We are striving for orthodoxy both in our *message* and in our *method*.

Someone once asked me, "What do you do differently today from what you used to do?"

I try to tell people how holy God is. Using the Word, I try to get them to see how sinful they are. Then I try to show them what God has done in love and grace for them, and what they must do in response to Him. Then I tell them, "When you do what God's Word commands you to do, you will be born again. And when you are born again, you will have the witness of the Spirit. When you know you have passed from death to life, you come and tell me."

You see, I cannot tell them they are born again. I'm too easy to convince. But the Spirit of God is Truth. He knows when one has passed from death into life. They will sense it *within*.

You may ask, "Isn't that emotion?" No. It is *knowing*. The same part of you that knows you're here and not somewhere else, also knows whether or not you are born of God.

If I were to ask—"Are you married?"—and you have to look for a wedding ring on your finger, or look for a marriage license, then I believe you have a problem.

If you are not sure you've been born of God, then you have a spiritual problem! It is very important to settle that question immediately. I would not rest until I had settled it and found out exactly what my state is.

I want to call your attention to Romans 15:13. It may seem that I'm giving you a Bible drill. But I think it is very good for you to see the scripture that is being referred to. It should be marked in your Bible, to indicate that you have been there, that you have visited that "address": "Now the God of hope fill you with all joy and peace in believing, that ye may abound in hope, through the power of the Holy Ghost."

One of the blessed fruits of being born of God is "joy and peace in believing." You will have the witness of the Spirit. The witness of the Spirit is not joy, nor is it peace. It is *knowing*. And knowing is a solid assurance that can never be shaken.

Witness of the Spirit:

1. What are some of the evidences that a person has been born of God?
2. Who is the only one capable of telling a person whether or not he's been born again? What happens when we assume this role?
3. In light of the Holy Spirit's path into the heart of a sinner—awakening, conviction, repentance, and heart faith—how would *you* determine whether or not someone you know is ready to pray and give his or her life to God?
4. What is the difference between "feeling" either excited or saddened by a gospel message and "knowing" that you are a child of God?
5. Read Galatians 5:16–25. Are there areas of your life that the Holy Spirit is speaking to you about when you read this passage?

A Mighty Fortress Is Our God

And tho this world, with devils filled,
Should threaten to undo us,
We will not fear for God has willed
His truth to triumph thru us.
The prince of darkness grim—
We tremble not for him;
His rage we can endure,
For lo! his doom is sure—
One little word shall fell him.

—Martin Luther

EIGHT

Temptation and Sin:

I Thought I Was a Christian

If we say we have no sin, we deceive ourselves, and the truth is not in us (1 John 1:8).

If we walk in the light as he is in the light, we have fellowship one with another (1 John 1:7).

Now are ye clean through the Word which I have spoken unto you (John 15:3).

We carry with us into the Christian life the same body we had before we were born again. We have been given the sure promise that we *will* have a glorified body when we see Him face to face—unfortunately, we have not received it yet.

A scar on your knee, from when you fell against the lawnmower last year, is still there the morning after you were born again. Likewise, there are various other *old* things that are with us as we enter the Christian life, including our appetites, drives, urges and old attitudes.

When God made us He gave us many different appetites—an appetite for food, because that's how we are to be sustained. He gave an appetite for knowledge, because that's how we learn, line upon line, precept upon precept, about God. He gave an appetite for status, because we are to rule over God's creation. He gave an appetite for pleasure, because God has given us so many marvelous things to enjoy. He gave us an appetite for sex as a means of increasing His family.

Have you ever considered how He painted the morning sunrise and the evening sunset? He didn't *have* to do that. It could have been gray. But He gave us fantastic colors to enjoy *and* the ability to recognize them. Many Christians have the wrong idea that we are supposed to look, act and think *gray* and that is holiness.

But God looked at the being He made and to whom He had given all these appetites and urges and said, "It is *good!*"

So there's nothing wrong with our appetites. He gave us adequate means by which they could all be satisfied within His will. In order to reveal His will and to guide us into real satisfaction, God gave prohibitions. He said, "You do not satisfy your appetites *this* way." He established laws and rules.

But when we repented of our sin and savingly received the Lord Jesus Christ, we entered into the Christian life *and* have brought with us our appetites for food, knowledge, pleasure, status and for sex. All the appetites we had before professing Christ, we have carried with us. We also brought along all of our learned ways of responding. Unfortunately, the habituated responses we developed in our days without Christ were formed by a self-seeking, sinful inner man. And it is said that when one does something over and over again, a path is traced in the brain between the cells, which creates the line of least resistance.

So here we are. We have been born of God. We have resolved: "God, I'm going to please You in everything. If You'll forgive me, I'll never do these things again. My purpose now is to please You." And the first thing we encounter is temptation.

Now *temptation* is not sin. Temptation is the proposition presented to the mind that you can satisfy a good appetite in a forbidden way. Temptation *leads* to sin.

Now, note this: Sin is the decision of the will. It is not the *gratifying* of an appetite. Sin is the *decision* to do it. He that hates his brother is already a murderer, says Jesus (see Matthew 5:22). Hatred is the intention to hurt and harm. The one who hates has decided to hurt.

In the same way, the one who has the mind to commit adultery is already guilty. The decision to do it—even before the act is complete, and before the opportunity has been presented—constitutes the essence of sin. Again, sin is the decision to gratify a good appetite in a bad way.

So you're a brand new Christian—and you're tempted. Maybe it has to do with some trait in your personality, because you've carried it as part of your baggage from the old life to the new. For example, you may be one who did not like criticism before you became a Christian. When anyone criticized you, you turned and really gave it to them.

Well, that's part of the life of which you have just repented, one of the things you promised your heavenly Father you would abandon in order to please Him. But now you have already encountered criticism and reacted wrongly to it, and God is displeased with you. What happened?

You made a habitual response. You were not aware that you have carried those old traits, tendencies and habituated responses with you.

Now there's all the difference in the world between sin in the life of a believer—one who is born again—and the individual who is a counterfeit, giving mere lip-service to Christianity. A child of God who sins did something he *hates*; he has done something he did not want to do. He was overtaken in the fog and led aside by his appetite. Nevertheless, he did it.

Scripture is very practical, direct and realistic. It says, "If we say that we have no sin, we deceive ourselves, and the truth is not in us" (1 John 1:8). So we *have* sinned, and God wants us to be completely honest about that with Him.

Do you know what happens when a child of God sins? I've heard people say, "Well, I'll lose my reward."

Friend, we will lose a lot more than our reward. We had better face it! A lot of things are going to happen to us between now and reward time. So it would be wise for us to get acquainted with God's Word on the matter, because it is very explicit about what takes place when a child of God sins.

The first thing that happens when a child of God sins is that our *fellowship with God is broken*. "But if we walk in the light, as he is in the light, we have fellowship one with another" (1 John 1:7). And John also says, "If we say that we have fellowship with him, and walk in darkness, we lie . . ." (v. 6). It is clear, then, that fellowship with Him is interrupted when a child of God sins. But if we've never had the witness of the Spirit and the joy and peace in believing through the power of the Holy Spirit—if we are merely the product of "easy believism"—we are never even going to *know* whether or not fellowship with God has been interrupted. We can't know, because we never had any fellowship.

Do you see how important it is that people should start out right? Do you see why we should understand that it is the Spirit of God who tells us that we have joy and peace in believing? That's our spiritual nervous system. If we don't have that, we're like lepers. A leper can put his hand in the fire and never flinch, because his nerves are dead. But when we have God's Spirit alive within, we know when fellowship is broken and when the Spirit is grieved.

The second thing that happens when a child of God sins is this: *prayers are not answered.*

In Psalm 66:18, David said: "If I regard iniquity in my heart, the Lord will not hear me. . . ." The thing that is grieving God has not yet reached my lips. I have not yet put my hand to it. But if I "cherish" it—if I've decided to do it no matter what God says about it—then God won't hear me. My prayer will go unanswered.

Peter said to husbands and wives not to fuss with one another. Don't argue. Live together in peace, *so that your prayers won't be hindered* (1 Peter 3:7).

How many families get to fussing and then wonder why their children have gotten all torn up by the Adversary! The parents wonder why their prayers for their children are not answered.

Third, when a child of God sins, *God won't use him.* Oh, we may go on "using" God. And for all that, people may never know the difference. But God won't use us, because Scripture says, "Be ye clean, that bear the vessels of the Lord" (Isaiah 52:11). When we tolerate in our heart and life anything that grieves God, whose name is holy, then we can be certain He won't use us.

F. B. Meyer illustrated this in his wonderful book *The Christ Life for The Self Life*. In it, he reports that he had bought one of the first fountain pens that came out in England. He would carry with him the pen, some steel points, a blotter and a little bottle of ink. A pen that had ink in it—what a great new idea! The only problem was, the ink not only came out of the point, but it leaked over everything else. So whenever Meyer would finish writing, his fingers were blue up to the second knuckle.

When an improved type of pen came along, he bought that one. He still kept his first fountain pen, but it was stored in a drawer. Whenever he would prepare for a trip, Meyer had a supply of pens to choose from and would reach into the drawer for pens to take with him. Now whenever he picked up that first fountain pen, he would shove it back into the drawer.

He wrote:

> If that little pen could talk, it might say something like this: "I wonder what's happened? Once I always went with him wherever he went. Once I knew his thoughts before others. Once he used me to communicate with people. But now I'm left in this drawer. My owner doesn't use me anymore. I wonder why?"

Meyer said, "Pen, I can't use you. Because every time I use you, you get me dirty."

Do you see this? God never uses the life that gets Him dirty. This is a hard saying, but one we must take to heart.

You see, God receives no glory from those whose lives are soiled by sin. In these days, evangelicals are under special scrutiny by the world because of men and women whose ministries have proven to be distortions of the truth of God. Christians should know it is the grace of God that brings things done in secret to light.

Therefore, rather than join in discussions about fallen church leaders, it would be well for each of us to intercede in prayer for tender souls who expected great things from those ministries that brought so much disenchantment to their lives. They have been misled. Now they have been abandoned and are in a state of confusion. Our prayer is that God will hear the cry of their troubled hearts. If they are seekers after truth, they will be found of Him and be taken into His fold.

Fourth, the believer who sins against God is described in Ephesians 4:27: Give no place to the Devil. The reason the scripture offers that warning is because, if you give place to the Devil, he will take it. And *you will become more prone to Satan's attacks.*

How do believers give place to the Devil? It's explained quite clearly in the Word of God: "The angel of the Lord encampeth round about them that fear him" (Psalm 34:7). It's like living in a yard surrounded by a high boarded fence. The dogs outside can't get in, because the fence is tight to the ground. In just that way, the angel of the Lord makes a fence around the believer, his family and loved ones, as well as the work of the ministry.

But when we give place to the Devil, it's as if you have gone up to that fence and deliberately kicked the boards loose. Now that loosened board is swinging on the upper nails, but it's open at the bottom. It no longer offers security against the Devil's dogs who love to go sniffing around those loose boards in a believer's life. Finding one, they push their way in—once inside they tear up everything.

But note the scripture: It is because of "the fear of the Lord" in our lives that His angel encamps about us. To fear the Lord is to hate evil. If we have come to the place where we no longer hate evil, if it is easy to tolerate in our lives anything that grieves God, then we can be certain the Devil's dogs will sneak in and tear up everything that's precious in our home and family.

Does that sound as though we have nothing to worry about until we get "over there"? Does that sound like the only thing that will be lost is a reward? To me, it sounds like we're in trouble if we permit unconfessed and unforsaken sin in our lives.

Chastened By God—The fifth thing that happens to a child of God when he permits sin in his life ought to tilt the balance, if there is still any question. We fall into the chastening hands of God.

"It is a fearful thing to fall into the hands of the living God" (Hebrews 10:31). To confirm this, I've got a few scars I could show you.

But there's something marvelous here that I would like to point out. I've heard people say, "I know some Christians who are living in sin, and *they're* not being chastened by the Lord." Oh no, you don't! All you know are those who *profess* faith in Christ.

Here's the secret: God never lays a finger on the Devil's family. But He chastens every child and scourges every son (see Hebrews 12:6). Because for God's children, this place is the only *hell* we shall ever know. When we die it will be heaven forever. But with the Devil's family, this world is all the *heaven* they are ever going to have. When they die, it will be hell forever.

So if, like Esau, they have traded their souls for a mess of pottage, God does not throw gravel in the soup to make their teeth grind on it. He won't do it, because they chose that life for themselves. Therefore, if you find someone living in sin and enjoying it and you don't think they are being chastened by the Lord, then you have met someone of whom God has said, "That person is not my child. He has not been born into my family."

So take a second look. For God's child, chastening is not pleasant. But it's a much more frightening thing to have God disown you, saying, "You're not mine."

I've just listed five effects of sin in the life of a Christian. Are you and I prepared to do something about this? Let's look into the Word at a wonderful verse—God's prescription for the problem: "Now ye are clean through the word which I have spoken unto you" (John 15:3).

"Clean because of the word. . . ." What is He referring to?

Though I have no exegetical support for this, I sense He's referring to the laver in the tabernacle in the wilderness. Inside the tabernacle's outer gate was the altar of burnt offering. Further on was the inner tent with the holy place—the holiest of all. And between the altar of burnt offering and the holy place was the laver. We do not know how large it was, because no dimensions have been given. But we have some idea of how the laver was made—it was made of brass, and the inside was flat and lined with mirrors. Then it was filled with water.

The laver had a two-fold function. First, it was to show the Levites and the priests where the soot and dirt was on their faces. Then it was to provide the means for washing away the dirt.

And the Lord Jesus said, "You are already clean because of the Word." Thus we expect the Word to have a two-fold function: to be a mirror to the soul that we may know what in us is grieving God; and to show us how to deal with that sin.

How do you use the Word as a mirror to your hearts? I've chosen just a few scriptures, though there are many others.

For example, here is one that acts like an X-ray machine, looking deep within our hearts: There are six things the Lord hates, seven that are detestable to Him (see Proverbs 6:16–19). Then comes the list: God hates pride, a lying tongue, hands that shed innocent blood, a scheming heart, eagerness to do evil, a false witness. And the thing He abominates above all others is to spread dissension among brothers.

Having read those words, let's continue looking into the mirror of the Word: "Who, knowing the judgment of God, that they which commit such things are worthy of death, not only do the same, but have pleasure in them that do them" (Romans 1:32). We are looking into the mirror of the Word in Romans, and we see that if we have permitted anything in our lives that makes people worthy of death, those five things we pointed out have begun to take effect. And what is causing the curse of sin? The mirror says, "Being filled with all unrighteousness, fornication, wickedness, covetousness, maliciousness; full of envy, murder, debate, deceit, malignity; whisperers . . . (Romans 1:29).

So we see that, in God's eyes, murder is placed right alongside envy and strife. And the list continues: gossiping, back-biting. The mirror of the Word places these right next to "God-haters." Now you would think that He would have better discernment than to place the "little white sins" right next to the "big black sins." But God heaped them all together.

What we have just read tells us that if we have permitted into our life anything that God hates—especially something He abominates—we are in big trouble.

Now the mirror, the Word of God, shows only what is there. But the Spirit of God never wants to depress us. His aim is to cleanse us. Whenever we sense we have grieved God, let us permit the Spirit of God to speak to our hearts and show us what it is He wants us to deal with. This is what we must do every day of our lives, because we are walking through a wicked world. We come to the mirror of God's Word, just as the Levites went to the laver before they entered the holy place. It is part of the continual process that will lead believers to knowing God's so great salvation.

One time I was at a camp meeting in western Pennsylvania, and I made the statement, "I'm sure everyone here went to the mirror before you came to church."

When the meeting was over, a boy of about twelve years old, with a dirty face, came up to me. He put his hands on his hips, looked me square in the eye and said, "Preacher, you were wrong today."

"I believe you," I said, "because I can see egg on your face from breakfast."

"Oh, that was from yesterday," he said.

How long has it been since you've been to the mirror of the Word and opened your heart to the Spirit of God to let Him search you?

It is the Word that shows our attitude, our relationship, our actions and motives. The Word shows the things we've said or done that have grieved God. It is the Word that reflects back to show where our need is.

Once we have discovered what it is that God is dealing with, the Word tells us explicitly how to deal with what is wrong: "For if we would judge ourselves, we should not be judged. But when we are judged, we are chastened of the Lord, that we should not be condemned with the world" (1 Corinthians 11:31–32). That doesn't mean you wait until somebody finds out and judges you, because if you do you're going to get a whipping.

He said, "Judge yourself." Don't wait. That means you go to the laver and see your smudged face. You've read the law to yourself. You say, "According to the Word of God, this is what I did."

So you are judging yourself, and I ask, "What are you going to do about it, friend?" Your response must be: "I was wrong. And I'll never do it again. I'm done."

Now that you have judged yourself and have

decided you are forsaking your wicked ways, the Word tells you exactly what else you are to do about it: "If we confess our sins, he is faithful and just to forgive us our sins, and to cleanse us from all unrighteousness" (1 John 1:9).

I want to tell you what confession is *not*. True confession does not occur when you are so tired and can barely wait to fall into bed, so you barely touch one knee to the floor and lightly say, "Dear Lord, if I've done anything wrong, please forgive me." That is not confession. To confess means to say with God what God says about our actions. Call the thing by its name—sin.

Some years ago, I had the privilege of being the evangelist at Houghton College, near Rochester, New York. We were in a revival meeting there, and God had visited us.

One evening, I gave an invitation and students filled the front rows. One young lady was sitting in the very front row of seats. Everyone else was pretty well dealt with, so I went to her and asked, "How can we help you?" As we knelt to pray, she told me about something that had happened the previous summer.

"Well, let's pray. You confess it to the Lord," I said.

While we were on our knees, she began to lecture God. She told Him how holy He was. He knew that. She told Him how wise He was. He knew that, too. Then she told Him how weak and frail people are. He knew all about that. After a while, I got tired. So I touched her on the shoulder and said: "When you've finished, turn out the lights. I'm going."

"What's the matter?"

"I know that it's probably beneficial to you to lecture God on all this. But we came here to pray and to confess."

"Oh, I'm getting around to it," she said.

"Well, you're not going to make it that way."

"Why not?"

"Because you're not willing to confess."

"What do you mean by that?"

"You must call the thing you did by its name— sin."

"Oh, I couldn't do that."

"Do you think God would be surprised?"

"But I can't tell that to God!"

"Well, then, goodnight."

"Don't go," she said.

"I don't want to go. I want to help you. But I can't unless you're willing to meet God on His terms. He said, 'If we confess our sin . . .' "

The young woman began to sob, and she finally confessed. That broke open the fountains of the deep, because she had been praying about the problem for six months and it had been tearing at her inside. But when she called the thing by its name, then she knew God had forgiven her. She knew she was forgiven and restored to fellowship in the church. But none of that happened *until* she had confessed.

At the time I was born of God, which I talked about earlier, we were living on a 360-acre farm. We would get up at 2:30 in the morning to go to the fields and work because that year, 1933, was a time of tremendous drought. I would go out to the barn and harness old Granny and Topsy, our two horses, and hitch them to a cultivator. Then I'd fill my two-quart Mason jar with water to take with me. Just as soon as I could spy the little green shoots of corn, it was my job to start down the field with the cultivator.

Then, at 6:00 in the morning, I'd come back into the barn, where my father, the hired man and I had to milk six cows. After that we would go into the house for breakfast. We tried to do all that and hurry back to the field by 7:00 in the morning.

On one particular day, my team of horses was so tired I brought them back from the field about 8:30. They weren't going anywhere. I set down my water bottle and was ready to do nothing but sit. Just then, my mother came out of the screened porch.

"Sonny, I'm so glad to see you," she said. "I've got two little errands I would like you to do for me."

I'd been up every morning at 2:30 and had been cultivating with two grown men. I was only 13 years old. And now here was my mother, wanting some errands done. So I did something I hope none of you know anything about. I sassed my mother. She was taken aback. When she spoke again, I sassed her again. After she spoke the third time, I added something cunning to my sassing.

My mother just looked at me. "Son," she said, "I thought you were a Christian." Then she turned and quietly walked into the house.

I tried to ignore what had just happened. Wasn't I justified? But as I went to the pump to fill my water jar and put one hand on the handle, I suddenly had to leave my Mason jar and run to the barn.

I ran in between the mangers and sobbed like a baby. Because, you see, I had just been born of God six weeks earlier and had determined I wanted to please God. I'd told Him I would obey Him. The thing He had used to show me that I was lost, in fact, was the way I had always dishonored and disobeyed my parents. And now I had just sassed my mother!

After a while, I stopped sobbing. In my ear, I heard the memory of a song we had sung at camp meeting: "Peace, perfect peace in this dark world of sin. The blood of Jesus whispers, peace within."

I sat there and confessed my sin over and over again. Then God spoke His forgiveness to my heart and I knew the blood of Jesus had cleansed me.

Then I went back to the house and asked my mother to forgive me. After that, I did the errands she had wanted done. When I filled my jar to go back to my team of horses, I went a wiser young man than ever before—because I realized I had carried into the Christian life a traitor who would betray me. My *self*.

When we're tempted and we sin, we have to deal with it. Whenever it occurs, we have to do our first works again. It is Jesus himself who prescribed it this way: ". . . you are clean through the Word." So learn to come to it daily. Make your salvation sure by steeping yourselves in the Word of God. Commune often with Him in prayer. Allow Him to direct you by His Spirit, step by step.

Whenever He shows you there is a need, judge it, confess it, forsake it, and know the cleansing of the precious blood of Jesus.

Temptation and Sin:

1. Are our desires sinful in and of themselves?
2. What is the difference between sin and temptation? Does sin always involve the "act"?
3. What five things happen when a child of God sins?
4. What is the "mirror" that believers should go to for cleansing?

All Things Are Possible

All things are possible to God;
To Christ the power of God in men;
To me when I am all renewed,
In Christ am fully formed again,
And from the reign of sin set free,
All things are possible to me.

—Charles Wesley

NINE

Victory:

Releasing the Power to Win

Now these things were our examples, to the intent we should not lust after evil things, as they also lusted. Neither be ye idolaters, as were some of them; as it is written, The people sat down to eat and drink, and rose up to play. Neither let us commit fornication, as some of them committed, and fell in one day three and twenty thousand. Neither let us tempt Christ, as some of them also tempted, and were destroyed of serpents. Neither murmur ye, as some of them also murmured, and were destroyed of the destroyer. Now all these things happened unto them for ensamples: and they are written for our admonition, upon whom the ends of the world are come. Wherefore let him that thinketh he standeth take heed lest he fall. There hath no temptation taken you but such as is common to man: but God is faithful, who will not suffer you to be tempted

above that ye are able; but will with the temptation also make a way to escape, that ye may
be able to bear it (1 Corinthians 10:6-13).

Everywhere I go, I meet people who want God
to give them such an experience with himself that
they'll never be tempted again. But, as I often tell
them, if you ever come to the place where you are
not subject to temptation, then you'll be holier
than our wonderful Lord. Because He was "in all
points tempted like as we are, yet without sin"
(Hebrews 4:15). Therefore, we need to be aware
that as long as we live we are going to be capable
of yielding to temptation.

Is there ever victory over temptation, then?

Yes! We read, "You shall call him Jesus, for he
will save his people from their sins." He saves—
not just from hell, which is the penalty of sin—
He saves His people from the *power* of sin. Therefore, we have to expect that in His work upon the
cross, our Lord included a means by which we
can escape and overcome temptation.

A few years ago, I was invited to speak in New
Hampshire at an InterVarsity Christian Fellowship retreat, where I had also spoken the year
before. Students from universities and colleges in
the Boston area had come together for a three-
day gathering. I arrived at a lovely inn on Friday
afternoon at about 4:00 P.M., and met a young
man who was at the piano trying to make some
music. He was not having much success at it, so

as I entered the room he stopped playing.

"I came a little early," he said, "so I would have a chance to talk to you."

"What is it you wanted to say?" I asked, as I dropped my bags and sat down beside him.

"I just wanted to warn you that if you're going to offer any of that victory stuff you gave us last year, I'd rather not hear it."

"Why is that?"

"Because it doesn't work."

"That's important to know," I said. "I'm glad you're here to warn me. But, if you don't mind, please explain what you mean."

"Well, last year you taught us that there is victory over temptation. There was a particular area in my life I was having problems with. After hearing you, I went back home excited, because I was sure I was going to be able to get victory over it. Well, I did what you told us to do—but it didn't work."

"What was it that you recall I had told you to do?"

"You gave us a verse—1 Corinthians 10:13. I memorized it. I said it over and over again. When I was tempted, I'd just quote that verse. I kept saying it again and again and again. But it didn't help at all."

I turned to the text in my Bible and let the young man read it aloud.

"What does it say?"

"That there will be 'a way of escape,' " he said.

"Yes, the Word says that there *is a way* of escape," I said. "But the *verse* is not *the way* of escape. Apparently, all you remembered was the verse. You didn't pay attention to what I said about Christ himself."

At the outset, we need to know that there are three major enemies that confront and attack us. They are *self*, the *world* and *Satan*.

Self—this is called "the old man." Paul spoke of it as "I." Your self is your worst enemy.

The world—this is the system in which we live and move, and it is organized by its own god. It has put forth every effort so that the gratifying of our appetites by evil means will look attractive, desirable and beautiful. Those efforts on the part of the world system are against the will of God and, moreover, the world system is totally arrayed against all the purposes you have formed in your heart to please God.

Satan—he is an ancient foe of the Lord Jesus Christ. Jesus called him "the prince of this world"—the one who was coming who had nothing in Him. Satan is also described as "the god of this world."

Now these three enemies assault us and give us problems. We would expect that if God is going to provide us with victory, it must address all of these enemies. You can be assured that God does give us a simple, practical and most effective way of dealing with all that these three enemies could bring against us.

First of all, however, you must recognize that no man is exempt from temptation and falling.

After I graduated from Bible school, I went as a missionary to Africa—to the Sudan. I'd been preparing so long and anticipating it so keenly that I was convinced when I placed my feet on the continent of Africa there would be a radical, saintly transformation in me.

I had not been great in prayer. But from that time on, I felt I would be a powerful intercessor. I had not been all that effective as a witness, but I was sure that when I hit African soil and drank African water, I would be the greatest of witnesses—so much so, that David Livingstone probably would have wished he had another chance.

Except that, traveling to Africa gave me a bad case of sea sickness. I was glad to be on dry land, so I could recover from the ravages caused to my body by the sea journey, but my attitude did *not* recover. Nor did Africa induce any great spiritual progress in me. When I got to the station of the White Nile, south of Khartoum, we began the actual work of missions. We had been assigned to the education department where we did a linguistics survey among tribes that had no contact with the gospel. It was hard work.

In Africa, I soon found I was not spending

much time in the Word or in prayer. I was not seeking God as I earlier had thought I would. I was thoroughly disappointed in myself. But I found a way to survive the discovery that I was not as spiritual as I knew I ought to be. I determined to prove that none of my colleagues were spiritual either. That meant I had to be discerning—that is, I had to have a critical mind, fed by an even more critical spirit. With all that equipment, it wasn't difficult for me to develop still another tool—a sharp, sarcastic tongue.

When someone put a little pressure on me for reasons I was certain were not fair, I would burst out with a few words that would cut them through and put them down. How I hurt people with my sarcasm! I had the idea I was God's little ice pick, assigned to breaking all the balloons around me.

But when I said something that hurt someone, I would have to go to my room in misery. I knew it was sin. I would get down on my knees and cry out to God, "Forgive me! Forgive me!" With gritted teeth and with my fingernails digging into the palms of my hands, I recall saying, "Oh God, if You'll forgive me, I'll never do it again." And He did forgive me.

But I did the same thing again and again.

I discovered that victory does not come from grinding your teeth, or by puncturing your palm with your fingernails. But at the time it was all I knew.

In Bible School, I was taught a course on "The Christian Life" and had gotten an A in it. But everything I learned was in my head. Truth had never migrated the necessary eighteen inches down into my heart. So there I was in Africa, boasting of an A in a course on Christian living, while realizing that I was a total failure as a Christian. I knew that by hurting my fellow missionaries I was grieving the Lord.

In due course, I returned to America on a furlough, determined never to go back to Africa. Further, I did not want to go on in the ministry unless I could find victory over my traits and tendencies—those habits of my mind and disposition that were leading me far from God. I had to find a way of victory over myself.

Seeking help, I went to a pastor in West Palm Beach, Florida, where my family was living.

The pastor said to me, "I think you need to go to seminary."

So I matriculated at a seminary in Louisville, Kentucky. I paid the tuition, bought my books, went to my room, and just sat there. After looking through the books on my desk, I realized I already had read half of them. And I didn't like what I read the first time. I didn't like the idea of being forced to study them.

Immediately, I knew that my need was never going to be met by what was being offered at the seminary. There was nothing wrong with the seminary, but it was not the right medicine for my illness.

The next day, I went back to the registrar's office and *de*-matriculated.

"We'll have to charge you a month's rent for the room," he said, which was all right with me, because I had gotten back most of my money.

"Then if you don't mind," I said, "I'll stay here a month and live out my rent."

During that month, I took a spiritual inventory of myself. I went back through the years. Back . . . back . . . all the way back. I found that in those years, I had collected all I'd learned from others. It was like picking leaves off other men's trees. My heart had become a theological compost pit, where dead leaves had been piled one upon another. Some leaves were still green, because they were truth. But even those few green leaves were not attached to me. They were just truth in the abstract.

"What's real?" I asked myself. "Where can I find reality?"

In memory, I traced my way back to South St. Paul—to the night I had knelt at that altar at the Red Rock Holiness Camp Meeting. That was the night I had opened my heart to Jesus Christ and I was marvelously born of God. He had given me the witness of the Spirit to my spirit that I was born again. I was His child. That was true.

I saw that the *last* real thing that had ever

happened to me with God was the *first* and only real thing that had ever happened to me with Him. From that time on, nothing but words had piled in on my mind. It was then I realized *how* I had gotten off on the wrong foot.

The day after I went to the altar at Red Rock, I went to the children's worker at the camp meeting. She was a wonderful woman of God and I wanted her to know about the marvelous thing that had happened to me.

"Last night, I was born again," I told her.

"Oh, that's nice, Sonny," she said. "Now you need to be sanctified. Let's go back into the auditorium and we'll pray."

So we went back into the auditorium where I had been the night before—to the very place where God had met me. She put words in my mouth and I prayed them.

In that moment, I went from reality—from revelation of God to my heart that I'd been born again—into presuming that, if I knew the words and could quote Scripture, then it was *mine*.

It was from that day on that I had been introduced to religious unreality. It was in my intellect; I assumed that if my mind *perceived* it, my heart had *received* it.

You see, that dear children's worker was so concerned about trying to bring someone who had just been born into the family of God into what she termed "sanctification," that she caused a short-circuit in my spiritual growth.

And so there I was, years later, in a room in Louisville, Kentucky. In my own eyes, I was a failure as a missionary. I had come to realize that the last real thing that had ever happened to me spiritually was the day when I was born of God!

I determined at that moment, as long as I live in the flesh—as long as God lets me breathe and walk on the topside of His green earth—I would make a clear distinction between what my mind perceives and what my heart has received and experienced. And I was determined never to confuse them.

As I mentioned, my family was at West Palm Beach and I was about to join them. But someone suggested, "Go by way of Clearwater, Florida. You can represent the Sudan Inland Mission at the conference there."

I drove down from Kentucky and arrived late at night. I went to the morning service and just sat listening to the speaker. I had never heard of him. In fact, I knew no one at all at the conference. But as I listened to the speaker, I thought, *"That man knows the Word."*

The rest of the day was spent talking with people and doing the things I was assigned to do as a missionary. Then that evening, when I heard the speaker again, I thought, "That man not only knows the Word, but He knows the *Lord.*"

So by the following morning, I was glad to

hear the speaker again, because I was now feeling warm and open toward him.

But he began to do something that I considered to be a bit cruel. I found that, though he had never heard of me, he must have known all about me. Because he was telling everybody in the auditorium about my failures, my problems and my difficulties. I had no idea who had squealed on me, but I can tell you that he had quit preaching and was deep into meddling! It was not the least bit pleasant for me.

By the evening service, things had developed from unpleasant to just plain miserable. So I found a place far in the back—way over on the right hand side of the auditorium.

But I was not prepared for that same speaker to put his arm halfway across the auditorium. He seemed to be wiggling his finger right under my nose, telling everyone there all about the problems I was having. I dropped my head, and let it hang on my chest. I certainly was not able to fight the man. He was absolutely right.

Then he asked a question: "Do you know what's the matter with you?"

I didn't know if I was supposed to break the silence and respond. But I felt like saying, "You're telling everything about me. Just go right ahead and tell all the rest." But I had sense enough to keep my big mouth shut. He had cut my sarcastic tongue quite short.

"This is your problem," the speaker went on. "When you came to Christ, you knew what you needed. You wanted to be forgiven and pardoned. You wanted to be born again. But your problem is that you were so interested in what *you* needed that you did not wait to see what *God* wanted for you."

That made sense to me, so I listened more intently.

"You went to the cross saying, 'Oh, God forgive me; pardon me. Give me eternal life.' And God did forgive you, pardon you and give you eternal life. But then you, the forgiven sinner, went in—as it were—and went right through the cross. Thus, the cross was behind you and the gates of heaven were before you. You began to run. And you have been tripping all over your feet ever since. You run, and then you trip. You get up and you have to go back and do your first work all over again. Run a little—fall. Run a little—trip and fall again. Haven't you gotten tired of this up-and-down thing? Don't you want to know why it's been like that?"

I listened eagerly.

"Your problem is you never turned around to look at the cross. Look again. You will find two people on that cross—Jesus Christ and you. He is there as your representative—the One who died in your place. He has identified himself so completely with you that He fulfilled the Word which says, 'The soul that sinneth, it must surely die.'

The Lord Jesus was there *as* you—*embracing you*, as it were. He was made to be what you were, so that in the eyes of God you were there with Him."

In that instant, a miracle happened. It was the first time in my entire Christian life that I had been in a situation where that kind of thing had happened. I was elated. For the first time, I found victory over criticism and sarcasm. Victory at last!

But a week or so later, somebody did something I didn't like and—well, I did it again. That's when I realized what Paul meant when he said, "I'm always being delivered up to death."

Nothing expresses this so well as the words of a favorite old hymn. We sing it, but I wonder if we know what we're singing:

> Moment by moment, I'm kept in His love;
> Moment by moment, I've life from above;
> Looking to Jesus till glory doth shine;
> Moment by moment, O Lord, I am Thine.
> Dying with Jesus, by death reckoned mine;
> Living with Jesus, a new life divine;
> Looking to Jesus till glory doth shine.
> Moment by moment, O Lord, I am Thine.

The songwriter is telling us that when we are under temptation, we are to go back to the cross and see ourselves crucified with Christ.

How grateful I am for George Mondell, pastor

of Maranatha Tabernacle in Upper Darby, Pennsylvania. For he was the speaker at that meeting in Florida where I was led up the road to victory. As long as I live I will be grateful that I discovered that the day Christ died for me I died with Him—and that He also died *as* me. I know now that there were two people on the cross—Christ and me.

You, too, can have victory at the moment of temptation. Your victory comes by *reckoning* yourself to be dead, indeed, to sin.

God's Word says, "Reckon ye also yourselves to be *dead* indeed unto sin, but *alive* unto God through Jesus Christ our Lord" (Romans 6:11).

If we exchange the word "reckon" for the word "consider," this may make it more understandable: *Consider* yourself dead to sin. Now a dead person can neither see, hear, feel or think. Things may occur around him, but for the dead person they no longer exist.

What is it that is breaking your peace and fellowship with God? Consider yourself dead to it. It does not exist for you.

But wait! That's not all. We are to consider ourselves dead to sin, and "alive to God." Thus declares the Word. A true Christian *is* dead to sin and the things of this world, and because he lives a resurrected life he is "alive to God through Jesus Christ our Lord."

Plain and simply, for the Christian, Christ is

his life. He (Christ) is the power who overcomes our trials and temptations in and around us. Whatever the thing may be, it is powerless before the powerful One who is the Way for us to victory.

I was speaking on this subject sometime later to members of the First Presbyterian Church in Flushing, Long Island. I had said, "If you'd like to have the victory, go into the prayer room and I'll join you."

About twenty-five people were there. Among them was Ronny Avelon, a singer who appears frequently in the New York area.

Among my remarks, I said to the group, "Between now and this time tomorrow night you're going to have a personal opportunity to test the truth of identification with Christ and victory through reckoning. So tomorrow, after the service, I invite all of you to come back. Let me know whether or not this truth works. I want you to be a walking sermon, so I won't fill your mind with theory."

The next evening, when the group returned, Ronny Avelon was there with his wife. He looked as though he had just had the greatest day of his life.

I must tell you that there was another singer well-known in the New York area by the name of Antone Marco. Now I had no idea that the one thing Ronny Avelon hated, more than anything else, was to be called by his rival's name. Whenever that happened he would become enraged.

That evening, as Ronny Avelon came up to me, I had a slight lapse of memory and said to him: "Well, Brother Marco, will you tell us what happened to you since we saw you last evening?"

I saw Ronny's eyes flash and the nape of his neck grow red. For a moment, he seemed to be wrestling inwardly. Then, he looked at his watch and said, "Well, you were right. Almost twenty-four hours have passed. You told us it would happen this way. And it did—with just three minutes to go!"

After that, Ronny went on to tell us what a great day he'd had. He was ready to tell how wrong I was, because he had not been tempted during the entire day. But then I had called him by his rival's name.

"I was about to explode," Ronny told us. "But then I saw myself on the cross with Christ. It *works*. There *is* a way of victory!"

Do *you* know how to release the resurrection life of Christ into your heart at the moment of temptation? Do you realize that these times of temptation and the testing of your faith are the preparation God has designed for you, so that you may go on to experience God's so great salvation?

You, too, will have an opportunity to test this truth in the next twenty-four hours. When temptation comes, I want you to have something that works.

When you discover that you are with Christ on the cross, God will give you the victory you have been looking for. And now, in Christ, it can be yours!

Victory:

1. What are the three major enemies that confront and attack us?
2. Will we ever be so spiritual that we cannot be tempted?
3. How do you "reckon," or consider yourself "dead" to sin? What does it mean to be "alive to God"?
4. What is the difference between "truth in the abstract" and truth that has become "real" in your life? How do you go about making the truths found in God's Word "real" in your life?